Public Speaking Course Guide
COMM 2004, Spring 2018

Ms. Brandi Quesenberry, Course Director and Editor
Dr. Marlene M. Preston, Course Designer and *Course Guide* Author
Department of Communication
Virginia Tech

	Page
Introduction	1
Course Basics, Part I, Overview	3
Syllabus	5
Course Basics, Part II, Student Growth and Performance	7
Course Basics, Part III, Connecting with Faculty and Students	9
Course Basics, Part IV, Evaluation Policies	10
Course Basics, Part V, Public Speaking & University Honor Code	13
Course Basics, Part VI, Calendar	15
Unit I -- Narrative Speech	17
Speech 1 Guidelines	18
Presentation Plan	21
Speech Critiques -- Providing and Receiving Feedback	23
Self-Assessment	35
Managing Course Responsibilities	37
Research Participation	38
Unit II -- Concept Speech	39
Speech 2 Guidelines	40
Presentation Plan	42
Critique forms	43
Unit III -- Progress Report	53
Speech 3 Guidelines	54
Presentation Plan	58
Critique forms	59
Unit IV -- Issue Analysis Speech (Perspectives)	69
Speech 4 Guidelines	70
Context Analysis; Organization	72
Presentation Plan	75
Critique forms	77
Unit V – Persuasive Group Speech	87
Speech 5 Guidelines	88
Presentation Plan	90
Critique forms	91
Appendix A: Supplementary Notes	101
Appendix B: Alternative to Research Participation	103
Appendix C: Course Development	107

With appreciation to Brandi Quesenberry, Graduate Teaching Assistants across the years, and countless undergraduates, who have maintained the integrity of the course and who have offered suggestions for enhancing this *Course Guide* each year.

Public Speaking Course Guide, Spring 2018
Copyright © 2018 by Marlene M. Preston

Requests for permission to make copies of any part of the work should be mailed to:

Permissions Department
Academx Publishing Services, Inc.
P.O. Box 208
Sagamore Beach, MA 02562

Printed in the United States of America

ISBN-13: 978-1-68284-392-5
ISBN-10: 1-68284-392-0

Public Speaking -- REAL PS

Welcome!

Public Speaking is required for students in many majors because ALL college students need excellent oral communication skills.

Academics -- In coursework across campus, students need to contribute in large lectures, present their research in classes or at conferences, and present their work in groups. If they continue to graduate school, the need for great speaking skills only increases.

Professions -- In every profession, college graduates need excellent communication skills. Just take a look at the classified ads; employers are looking for new employees who are well trained in their disciplines and who can communicate that knowledge to clients and peers.

Citizenship -- Those same skills are necessary for effective participation in the community -- for a presentation to City Council, a fund-raising appeal for the PTA, or a protest to the judge when a speeding fine has been imposed!

Because of these REAL academic, professional and societal demands, Public Speaking has always been an important course. This *Interchange* model for teaching and learning in Public Speaking helps students meet those demands in a learning environment that honors their time, makes the most of technology, and maximizes opportunities for practice and presentation.

Highlights of the course structure:

- Emphasis on public speaking beyond the classroom -- REAL PS
- Hybrid of online instruction and in-class practice
- Use of basic speech models with increasing complexity across the semester
- Use of accessible textbook that focuses mostly on practical application
- Development of a Canvas site for use by all sections of Public Speaking, thus assuring consistency across sections in delivery of instructional material and assessment
- Acknowledgement of students' expertise and familiarity with technology, allowing them access on their own schedules to course materials
- Use of class time for students to develop and practice speeches in a small-class setting, thus building competence and confidence

This *Interchange Model* of Public Speaking is designed to meet needs of students, departments, and the institution as we prepare students to continue their paths into their academic and work lives with enhanced communication skills.

Student Needs and Responsibilities

In order to assure your success in this course, please recognize your obligation to be in class when we DO have class! <u>We offer online instruction instead of a large lecture in order to make the course more convenient and effective for you</u>. However, that means that our in-class days are limited and precious! You need to be in class when class is scheduled and to pay careful attention to online assignments when you are not scheduled to be in class. We don't have extra time to repeat information, manage late work, or schedule make-ups for missed speeches. Our in-class time will be carefully structured to maximize support for your speech development and presentation. Please pay close attention to the schedule and respond carefully to assignments.

Please note: This *Course Guide* contains course policies, strategies for your success, and the details for each assignment. Take every opportunity to familiarize yourself with the course expectations so that you can achieve at whatever level you want!

Course Focus -- REAL PS

When students plan to take Public Speaking, they sometimes think of the course as merely something to endure because it's a requirement. They expect to get through the assignments, take the final exam, and escape.

Actually, the study of public speaking is important far beyond the simple meeting of a requirement. Presenting ideas to others in formal settings is a crucial part of academic and professional life. Your success hinges not only on your knowledge of your major, but also your ability to present that knowledge to others.

That real-life application in this course is emphasized through a thread identified as **REAL PS**. Every speech you develop for this class and for other speaking situations demands your attention to **R**esearch, **E**thics, **A**nalysis, and **L**anguage/Listening. You will be completing activities, watching sample speeches, and considering your own speech development in the light of these speech components.

The following topics are part of the **REAL PS** thread that is woven through the units of this course:

Research --
- Generating detail from personal experience
- Combining personal expertise with authoritative source
- Identifying appropriate and credible library sources
- Researching various perspectives
- Considering primary and secondary research in academic and professional speaking
- Providing appropriate bibliography and oral citations of sources

Ethics --
- Emphasizing personal credibility
- Avoiding plagiarism in PS
- Informing audience of vulnerable non-experts
- Building an argument
- Balancing personal goals with audience needs (classmates, clients) in informative and persuasive speaking

Analysis --
- Considering personal confidence and competence
- Analyzing speech context: setting, audience, occasion
- Identifying audience needs
- Analyzing argument

Language/Listening --
- Listening to fellow speakers with an open mind
- Critical listening and feedback
- Listening and to prepare for Q & A
- Listening for unacknowledged bias
- Selecting language appropriate for purpose and context

Course Basics, Part I -- Course Overview

Public Speaking (COMM 2004) is important for your academic and professional success! This course is designed to help you build skills in your communication with audiences--whether they are your classmates, clients or fellow citizens.

The *University Course Catalog* includes this COMM 2004 description: "Basic skills of public speaking; speech organization and delivery; emphasis on in-class delivery of speeches."

You've probably had some experience with speaking in public, such as presenting a report to the members of a club or accepting a trophy at a sports banquet. This course will help you to build skills and confidence as you explore strategies for creating and delivering effective speeches.

Learning Goals

Your learning goals are important, and you might have goals that reach beyond those listed here. Certainly your speaking skills will continue to grow across a lifetime of practice. The following list of goals is taken from the National Communication Association's list of competencies for undergraduates in any major. You should be able to demonstrate the following competencies by the time the term has ended:

- Determine the purpose of oral discourse in various contexts
- Choose a topic and restrict it to meet the needs of purpose and audience
- Construct effective message content
- Demonstrate effective delivery strategies
- Design and implement effective presentation aids
- Listen critically to understand and evaluate messages
- Recognize and employ ethical strategies in communication
- Identify strategies to reduce apprehension

Class Format -- The Interchange Model

This course is conducted partly in the classroom and partly online within Canvas. Your instructor will explain the ways in which the course is designed to be as engaging and flexible as possible. You will receive a schedule of online opportunities and in-class opportunities, which together require the amount of time you might formerly have spent entirely in the classroom.

To achieve learning in this hybrid format, you commit to being prepared for and attentive in class some days so that you can do work out of class on other days. Your engagement and preparedness are crucial! If we met in a large-lecture format, you would spend 3 hours a week in class and approximately 6 hours a week out of class to prepare your assignments. *With the Interchange Model, you'll spend lots less time in the classroom, but the number of hours you should commit to your work will not change.*

Organization, motivation, and strong time-management skills are necessary for your success in this course. Commit to this course, and you will reap lifelong benefits.

For more information about the Interchange Model, see the Appendix.

Public Speaking -- Formal Speeches

	Speech 1	Speech 2	Speech 3	Speech 4	Speech 5
Complexity	Level 1	Level 2—includes level 1	Level 3 – includes 1 and 2	Level 4 – includes 1-3	Level 5—includes 1-4
Type	Narrative -- extemporaneous	Concept -- extemporaneous with cited sources	Progress Report-- extemporaneous + cited sources	Issue Analysis-- extemporaneous with cited sources	Persuasive Group – extemporaneous + cited sources
Time	2½-4½ minutes	3½-5 ½ minutes	4½-6 minutes + Q&A	6½-7½ minutes	7½-8½ mins.
Topic choice/focus	Personal story with autobiog. significance	Concept or program related to higher ed or major	Project in which student is or has been involved; or local project	Controversial topic based on interest, major, or experience	Controversial topic based on group interest or experience
Audience	Classmates; analysis -- age	Classmates or peers in major	Audience who needs information about project	Audience in need of info. about the controversy	Audience open to persuasion
Purpose	Inform; socialize	Inform	Inform	Inform	Persuade
Credibility	Personal integrity; sincerity	Personal expertise as student and minimal research	Personal expertise and research from local sources and library databases	Variety of types of sources, including library databases	Variety, including personal experience and research from local sources
Support	Illustration, narrative	Definition, analogy, example; source citation	Examples, testimony, facts, statistics; source citation	Examples, testimony, facts, statistics; source citation	Examples, testimony, facts, statistics; source citation
Organization	Chronological order	Topical or spatial; Emphasis on intro and trans	Chronological; topical; Emphasis on conclusions	Cause-effect; problem-solution; topical	Cause-effect, problem-solution, or Monroe's M.S.
Voice & language	Vocal clarity and volume	Vocal variety	Language	Appropriate vocal variety and language choices	Appropriate vocal variety & persuasive language
Physical behaviors	Eye contact; posture; use of speaking notes; facial expression	Movement; gestures; variety of facial expression	Management of technology; variety of physical strategies	Mastery of technology; variety of physical strategies	Mastery of technology; group interaction & transitions
Presentation aids	Object; appearance	1-2 PowerPoint slides to enhance speech – image only	2-4 PowerPoint slides to enhance speech	4-6 PowerPoint slides (advanced)	4-6 PPT slides + spacer slides; min. 1 per person
Confidence	Addressing apprehension	Minimizing apprehension	Building confidence	Building confidence	Demonstrating confidence

Syllabus

Specific dates and other requirements will be announced in class and posted on Canvas.

Units	Reading Assignments	Evaluation	Points
Course Intro & Unit I	**Course Guide -- Intro materials and Unit I** Ch. 1-4 – Speaking, Managing Anxiety, Listening Ch. 13 – Outlining Ch. 18 – Vocal delivery Sample speeches – p. 27 O'Hair and Canvas site		
	Course Guide, Ch. 1-4, 13, 18, sample speeches	Unit I Quiz	100*
	REAL PS 1; Online and in-class activities	Participation	90
		Speech #1 -- Narration	180
Unit II	**Course Guide – Unit II** Ch. 7 & 8 -- Topic, Purpose, Support Ch. 10 & 11– Citing Sources & Organization Ch. 14 – Introductions Ch. 19 -- Delivery Sample Speeches--Canvas and p. 208 O'Hair *(Note--Parts of Ch. 6, 12, 20, & 23 addressed now but not on quiz.)*		
	Course Guide; Chapters 7, 8, 10, 11, 14, 19; p. 208; sample speeches	Unit II Quiz	100*
	REAL PS 2; Online and in-class activities; Midterm assess	Participation	90
		Speech #2 -- Concept	220
Unit III	**Course Guide – Unit III** Ch. 5 & 6 – Ethics & Audience Ch.15 & 16—Conclusions & Language Ch. 21-22 -- Presentation Aids Appendix E: Handling Questions Sample speeches--Canvas and p. 333 O'Hair		
	Course Guide; Chapters 5, 6, 15, 16, 21, 22 and App. E; sample speeches	Unit III Quiz	100*
	REAL PS 3; Online and in-class activities	Participation	90
		Speech#3-Progress Report	250
Unit IV	**Course Guide – Unit IV** Ch. 9 -- Credible research Ch. 12 -- Organization Ch. 17 -- Delivery Ch. 20 –Presentation Aids Ch. 23 -- Informative Speech Ch. 25 -- Argument Sample speeches--Canvas and p. 463 O'Hair		
	Course Guide (point & block organizational patterns); Chapters 9, 12, 17, 20, 23, 25; p. 463; sample speeches	Unit IV Quiz	100*
	REAL PS 4; Online and in-class activities	Participation	90
		Speech #4-Issue Analysis	300
Unit V Persuasion	**Course Guide – Unit V** Ch. 24--Persuasive Speech Ch. 26-- Organizing Ch. 27—Special Occasion Ch. 28—Online Pres. Ch. 29--Presenting in Groups Ch. 30—Professional Pres.		
	Course Guide; Chapters 24, 26, 27, 28, 29, 30	Unit V Quiz	100*
	REAL PS 5; Online and in-class activities; Research participation	Participation	90
		Speech#5 – Persuasion	100
Exam	*Cumulative*	Final exam	100
		Total	*2000*

Speeches: 53%; Participation: 22%; Quizzes and Exam: 25%

*Note – Out of 5 quizzes listed, the <u>lowest quiz grade will be dropped</u>; 4 quizzes count toward grade.

Course Materials -- The course was carefully designed to provide support for your learning and performance. The textbook, Canvas site, and in-class sessions were created to meet your needs as online learners of basic speaking principles and in-class speakers.

<u>**Texts.**</u> Be sure to keep up with the reading assignments for this class because your effective performance should include attention to strategies in the text. Beyond the textbook, you should pay careful attention to all email correspondence, Discussion Board postings, announcements, and unit introductions. Always read carefully and critically!

1. *A Speaker's Guidebook: Text and Reference* by Dan O'Hair, Rob Stewart, and Hannah Rubenstein (VT custom, 6th edition) -- The easily accessible text was also chosen so that you can use it as a reference when you have other academic or professional speaking obligations.

2. *Fall 2017 Course Guide for Public Speaking* by Dr. Marlene Preston

<u>**Course folder.**</u> Purchase an inexpensive pocket folder for use in submission and collection of speech materials.

<u>**Computer access.**</u> To participate fully in the course, you will need computer access so that you can (1) engage in electronic communication, (2) refer to the course Canvas site, and (3) explore electronic information sources. Your instructor may ask you to bring a laptop to class for in-class writing or research activities. Your instructor may also ask you not to use your laptop in class, unless instructed to do so. In conjunction with the *Course Guide,* this Canvas site will provide all of the information you'll need. If you have a question, check these resources first, and then contact your instructor if you are still in doubt. In order to gain the flexibility of controlling your own learning time online, you'll need to take responsibility for accessing the abundance of materials provided. Please get in the habit of checking Canvas often for messages from your instructor and the Course Director.

Other Resources
1. Online text site: www.bedfordstmartins.com/speakersguide/
2. Launchpad: www.launchpadworks.com
3. CommLab, a resource for student speakers who want to prepare and/or rehearse their speeches: www.commlab.vt.edu
4. Newman Library: www.library.vt.edu

Inclement Weather -- If the University is closed due to inclement weather, assignments scheduled for that day will be due at the subsequent class. Check your Canvas site for additional directions and assignment updates.

Accommodations -- If you have a documented learning or speaking disability, please inform your instructor within the first week of classes. Your instructor will arrange for accommodations as recommended by Services for Students with Disabilities office.

Units and Course Evaluation -- Following is a list of the units that will be discussed during this term. Each unit addresses various strategies related to message construction and delivery.

- REAL PS-- A semester-long unit integrated into each assignment, addressing the overarching principles of public speaking as they are found in higher education and in the professions: Research, Ethics, Analysis, and Language/Listening.
- Unit I -- Narration*
- Unit II -- Concept*
- Unit III -- Progress Report*
- Unit IV -- Issue Analysis – Perspectives*
- Unit V – Persuasive Group Speech
- Quizzes and Final exam

*Note: <u>All individual speeches must be presented in order to pass the class</u>.
Final grades for the course will be determined using this grading scale, based on the percentage of possible points achieved:

A = 93-100%   A- = 90-92
B+ = 88-89   B = 83-87   B- = 80-82
C+ = 78-79   C = 73-77   C- = 70-72
D+ = 68-69   D = 63-67   D- = 60-62   F = 59 and below

For more detail about grading policies, see Course Basics, Part IV.

Course Basics, Part II -- Student Growth and Performance

Information below will help you identify the goals for your growth as a speaker in this class. Of course, the class also includes other types of student contributions; standards for presenting your work are also included.

Student Growth as a Speaker -- This course will certainly help you build your speaking skills, and you may have the idea that you have a lot to accomplish or that you are an accomplished speaker already. If you've had speaking experiences in the past, you should build on those as you develop or refine skills in the following "canons of rhetoric," which have been acknowledged to be important in public speaking since the 5th century B.C.:

1. Invention   2. Arrangement   3. Style   4. Memory   5. Delivery

People who take Public Speaking should finish the course with at least basic competencies in these areas. (We'll be discussing them in detail in class and addressing them in out-of-class assignments.) Of course, you can achieve other levels of sophistication and accomplishment depending on your starting point and your own determination to improve. The course is designed with an emphasis on the same competencies for each speech, but with increasing levels of complexity. You and your instructor can work together to help you to achieve competence and confidence.

The course is structured around the delivery of four major speeches that will help you to build your speaking skills. Each will be accompanied by reading and assignments that will alert you to the subtleties of content development, organization, and delivery. This *Course Guide* includes detailed assignments, outline templates, and critique forms so that you'll have everything you need at your fingertips.

Student Growth through Formal Writing -- Written work will help you to organize and document your speeches, and it will assist you in processing information and reflecting on various standards for public speaking. Just as presentation is a component of speaking, it is also a component of writing. Readers make assumptions about your preparedness and your credibility based on the accuracy and style of your presentation. Whether you're submitting presentation plans or bibliographies, your work must include the following components:

- **Appropriate content** meets the requirements of the assignment and reflects critical thinking on your part.
- **Specific details** support your main ideas by clarifying or expanding. Help your reader to get a clear picture!
- **Logical organization** helps a reader follow your train of thought. Presentation plans must be organized according to the directions provided for each assignment.

- **Presentation** includes correct grammar and usage, effective style, and appropriate language choices. Presentation also refers to the format you use for written work -- standard font (size 12), one-inch margins all around.
- **Documentation** (if necessary) should be evidenced in two ways: oral citation and bibliography in correct MLA or APA form. When in doubt, document! Don't risk an Honor Code violation by incorporating another author's work into your own without citing it appropriately.
- **Submission** of materials should occur either in class (hard copy) or through Canvas. Include your name as part of the file name as shown on YOUR computer. That way, the file received by your instructor will show your name in the file.

Participation -- Informal Writing and Speaking -- During each week of the term, assignments will include various in-class and online activities, all of which are designed to enhance learning of the course materials. Because of the importance of this work, your participation is a significant portion of your final grade!

    In-class activities and homework. You might be assigned responsibilities such as bringing outlines to class, writing critiques of other speakers, delivering impromptu speeches, or reporting from groups.

    Online activities. Online activities might reinforce the day's class or they might underscore assigned reading. You might critique a sample speech, record practice speeches, analyze the ethical considerations in your own work, or apply the assigned reading to the development of one of your speeches.

Submitting Quality Work -- Whenever you have such worked assigned, it must be submitted by the posted deadlines as shown on Canvas. Your careful and thoughtful work will help you to master the material, succeed on the quizzes, and build effective speeches. Ask yourself:

- Does my response address all aspects of the assignment?
- Does my response reveal my understanding of the text or the in-class discussion?
- Does my response reveal my critical thinking about the subject?
- Is my response formatted correctly?
- Is my response intelligible to a reader and labeled appropriately?

Your Time Contributions -- Any homework or online assignments are designed to enhance your learning. They are planned to meet the requirements of a standard 3-credit course. Because students don't meet in the classroom 3 hours each week, these assignments help to provide instruction, examples, and application. Your completion of this work outside the class allows us to provide a course structure with part of the coursework online and part in a classroom.

    The assignments are based on the standards of higher education--2-3 hours outside class for every hour in. To do well in this course, you should expect to dedicate the same 3 hours you would have spent in class for any 3-credit class PLUS at least 6 hours outside of class for reading and homework.

Prepare -- Mark up your text and *Course Guide* as you read the information before the related class meeting, and bring those materials to class. You'll need to refer to your course materials during class, and you can annotate them with tips from your instructor.

Course Basics, Part III -- Connecting with Faculty and Students

Respect, respect, respect! Just as you would treat colleagues in the workplace or classmates in a classroom, your faculty and colleagues in this course also deserve your respect. Practice your communication skills whenever you post a message or send an email. Your tone should be friendly and professional.

Quality Engagement

Respect also involves providing quality work for others to receive and respond to. Don't waste the time of your classmates or faculty by submitting work you haven't spent any time developing. Engage in the conversation and the presentations with enthusiasm and depth.

You will also be providing feedback to peers about their work. Please offer constructive criticism so that your classmates can recognize what they did well when they gave their speeches and what they might do to improve for the next time. Provide meaningful and tactful comments. Give the kind of help you'd like to receive.

Punctuality

1. Attending class on time is particularly important because of the design of our class. When we are scheduled to be in the classroom, we'll be developing or presenting speeches. Speakers and audience members need to be ready at the start of class so that we can make the most of our time together.

2. Submitting work online or in class also requires punctuality. Instructors are committed to evaluating work promptly and help you to be ready for the next assignment. If you stay on schedule, you'll be ready! Of course, written work may be submitted late (with penalties as described in another part of this syllabus); however, the evaluation of that work will also be delayed because your instructor is keeping up with the submissions of the class.

3. Email exchanges also hinge on punctuality. If you have a question or concern, please let your instructor know immediately. Likewise, your instructor will respond as soon as possible on weekdays during normal working hours. Although you may have sent email at 2 a.m., you can't expect your instructor to respond until the next day -- probably after classes are over for the day.

Contacting with Faculty

If you have questions about the directions or expectations for an assignment. . .
- Review the information in this *Course Guide* and on the Canvas site.
- Check with classmates in your groups.
- Send email to your instructor or visit during office hours.

If you have a question about a grade. . .
- Review the grading criteria for the particular assignment.
- Review comments you received as feedback from instructor and peers.
- Send email to your instructor, asking your instructor to review the taped speech with you for further clarification.

If you have an illness or a personal problem, contact your instructor as soon as possible. You'll receive specific advice from your instructor about the best avenues for contacts. If you DO leave a phone message, please leave a local number so that your call can be returned.

Course Basics, Part IV -- Evaluation Policies

This course is designed to foster your success in this course and in your future experiences with public speaking. Consequently, you have many opportunities to demonstrate your understanding of the principles associated with public speaking and also your skill at making presentations. Your participation in the course is crucial to your growth AND to our ability to offer part of this course online. Those assignments allow you to accumulate lots of points -- points that you can control with your good work.

Please don't minimize that benefit. If you assume that 5% doesn't count for much in terms of your whole grade, just try factoring in some D's or F's that count as 5%; you'll quickly see that any low grades for participation can accumulate negatively to diminish your final grade.

The policies described here are designed to foster timely submission of quality work. Because of limited time in class, student learning will be optimal only if you keep on schedule and prepare assignments as indicated.

You may want to refer to other files for specific grading information. The grading criteria for assignments can be found in the files explaining those assignments. The weights for the various assignments and the grading structure are listed in the syllabus.

Attendance

The design of this class is dependent on your in-class participation and contribution. <u>Since much of the course material is provided online, our time together in class is precious.</u> Because this is a performance class, you need to have an audience when you give a speech, and you need to be part of the audience when others speak. While there is not a specific penalty for missing class, the in-class activities do yield participation points and can't be made up at a later date. If you have an illness or emergency documented through the office of your Dean, your instructor will do everything possible to help you maintain good grades.

Note: Excuses are provided through the Student Health Center or the Dean's Office when you have to miss all of your classes because you are hospitalized, have a severe illness, experience a death in the family, or have some other trauma. Any of these must be documented. Take your official doctor's note, hospital information, or other documentation to your dean. Begging your dean for an excuse because you didn't feel like giving your speech or lying about an illness is unethical and wastes everyone's time. In those cases, you might be subject to action by the University Honor System.

Due Dates -- Check Canvas for due dates and any updates.

> **Written work:**
> - **Informal written work (online or in-class submissions)** are due as discussed in class and noted in Canvas. Make back-up copies of your work!
> - **Formal written work**, such as speech presentation plans, must be submitted by dates assigned.
> - **Late submissions of written work**--such as homework activities, drafts, personal progress assignments--may be accepted with a penalty of a letter grade each day the assignment is late. *Note: Final outlines and critiques of others' speeches must be submitted as assigned; no late submissions are accepted.*
>
> **Spoken work:**
> - **Informal speaking (in-class).** In-class activities (group work, impromptu speeches) are designed to provide practice opportunities and cannot be made up at a later date.

- **Formal speeches (in-class).** Speeches must be presented on the days assigned. Presentation plans or bibliographies are submitted on speaking days and must be available before a speech can be presented. Due to the constraints of scheduling, class time is not available for make-up speeches. *Note: All individual formal speeches must be presented in order for a student to pass the class.*

Quizzes. All quizzes are offered online at the Canvas site. They are designed to help you master the material *before* you give a speech and to locate material for later use. Consequently, they are multiple-choice and open book. The quizzes are usually available at the time you would normally be scheduled for class so that the times are already scheduled in your planner.

Make-up quizzes are not available unless a student has an excused absence from the Dean's Office. If a make-up quiz is approved, the instructor will determine the deadline for taking that quiz; students will take a closed-book, hard-copy quiz that may combine multiple-choice and essay questions.

The lowest of the 5 quiz grades will be dropped so that only 4 quiz grades count toward the final grade.

Speech Presentation

Recording. All speeches will be recorded for later review by the instructor.

Time limits. The criteria for each speech include time limits. These limits are imposed so that (1) you can practice adjusting your presentations to various speaking constraints, and (2) you can be assured of having enough time within a given class period for your speech. In any professional setting, speakers must respect the boundaries imposed by bosses, audience members, clients, or schedulers. (If several students used more than the time allotted for their speeches, then someone would be deprived of the opportunity to speak as scheduled.)

Note -- Time Penalty. **Failure to meet the time requirement by a minute more or less will result in deduction of a letter grade from your speech.** Lesser problems with time limits will be penalized by ½ letter grade. Of course, any significant reduction in a grade is rarely necessary. Students who prepare carefully have no trouble with the allotted time.

Grading and Feedback -- Formal Presentations

Grades. Student work will be graded as quickly as possible, and grades will be posted on the Canvas site. You will never have to present a subsequent speech before the previous speech has been graded.

Feedback. Your instructor will provide a grade and comments about the strengths of your work and suggestions for improvement. You will also receive feedback from peers. Please review these comments carefully and use them to improve your speaking skills.

Clarifying feedback. If you would like to review the video of your speech with your instructor, please make an appointment to do so *before* the next speech is due. During this consultation session, your instructor will elaborate on the strengths and weaknesses of your presentation and answer any questions you may have about your grade.

Grading Criteria for Formal Assignments

Consider the following criteria as you review your graded work. Of course, graded work will be accompanied by notes from your instructor, indicating the strengths of your oral or written presentation and suggestions for further development of your skills. Seek clarification of these comments if you have questions.

Average Presentation "C"	Good Presentation "B"	Superior Presentation "A"
1. Format: conforms to the assignment's length and format	**1. Format:** conforms to the assignment's length and format	**1. Format:** conforms to the assignment's length and format
2. Organization: exhibits appropriate organization	**2. Organization:** exhibits appropriate organization	**2. Organization:** exhibits appropriate organization
3. Accuracy: appropriate language and correct grammar	**3. Accuracy:** includes appropriate language and correct grammar	**3. Accuracy:** includes appropriate language and correct grammar
4. Support: demonstrates competent use of supporting data	**4. Support:** demonstrates competent use of supporting data	**4. Support:** demonstrates competent use of supporting data
5. Outline: accompanies correctly formatted outline (and bibliography if necessary)*	**5. Outline:** accompanies correctly formatted outline	**5. Outline:** accompanies correctly formatted outline
	6. Style: arouses audience interest and understanding through appropriate style and expression	**6. Style:** arouses audience interest and understanding through appropriate style and expression
	7. Visuals: designs and incorporates effective visuals	**7. Visuals:** designs and incorporates effective visuals
	8. Logic: establishes supported and documented logic and reasoning	**8. Logic:** establishes supported and documented logic and reasoning
	9. Credibility: enhances the presenter's credibility as a competent and dynamic speaker	**9. Credibility:** enhances the presenter's credibility as a competent and dynamic speaker
		10. Creativity: constitutes a genuinely individual, creative contribution
		11. Rhetoric: achieves a skillful mastery of rhetorical concepts
		12. Language: vivid and precise

*Note: Required paperwork reflecting your preparation for a speech is generally valued 10% of the whole speech grade.

Grading and Feedback -- Informal Assignments

For informal writing in class, homework, or online assignments, your work will be evaluated by your instructor as he or she looks for the criteria shown on the table below.

Missing (F), **U**nsatisfactory (D), **S**atisfactory (C), **G**ood (B), or **E**xcellent (A).

	M	U	S	G	E
Match of student's response to assignment					
Connection of response to text or classroom discussion					
Evidence of student's critical thinking					
Correct format					

Points or letter grades will be assigned based on these criteria and the specific information required in each assignment. For example, if you score "good" on most of the criteria, you'll earn a "B." In some cases, work may be submitted late; posted grade penalties will apply. However, in-class activities cannot be made up at a later date. You can monitor your participation grade across the term by checking the Gradebook on Canvas. Please see your instructor if you have questions about that grade.

Course Basics, Part V --
Public Speaking and the University Honor Code

Honesty in your academic work makes you a trustworthy member of the class and also builds ethical habits for your professional career. Thoroughly review the following sections about the University Honor System and plagiarism to familiarize yourself with the possible problems.

University Honor System

As a participant in this class, you are bound by the Virginia Tech Honor System. The honor code will be strictly enforced in this course. All assignments submitted shall be considered graded work. All aspects of your coursework--online quizzes, homework, speech content, and in-class work--are covered by the honor system.

Please review the following statement about the Honor Code from the Virginia Tech Undergraduate Honor System (found at http://www.honorsystem.vt.edu/ The Undergraduate Honor Code pledge that each member of the university community agrees to abide by states:

> "As a Hokie, I will conduct myself with honor and integrity at all times. I will not lie, cheat, or steal, nor will I accept the actions of those who do."

Students enrolled in this course are responsible for abiding by the Honor Code. A student who has doubts about how the Honor Code applies to any assignment is responsible for obtaining specific guidance from the course instructor before submitting the assignment for evaluation. Ignorance of the rules does not exclude any member of the University community from the requirements and expectations of the Honor Code.

Commission of any of the following acts shall constitute academic misconduct. This listing is not, however, exclusive of other acts that may reasonably be said to constitute academic misconduct. Clarification is provided for each definition with some examples of prohibited behaviors in the Undergraduate Honor Code Manual located at https://www.honorsystem.vt.edu/

A. CHEATING

Cheating includes the intentional use of unauthorized materials, information, notes, study aids or other devices or materials in any academic exercise, or attempts thereof.

B. PLAGIARISM

Plagiarism includes the copying of the language, structure, programming, computer code, ideas, and/or thoughts of another and passing off the same as one's own original work, or attempts thereof.

C. FALSIFICATION

Falsification includes the statement of any untruth, either verbally or in writing, with respect to any element of one's academic work, or attempts thereof.

D. FABRICATION

Fabrication includes making up data and results, and recording or reporting them, or submitting fabricated documents, or attempts thereof.

E. MULTIPLE SUBMISSION

Multiple submission involves the submission for credit—without authorization of the instructor receiving the work—of substantial portions of any work (including oral reports) previously submitted for credit at any academic institution, or attempts thereof.

F. COMPLICITY

Complicity includes intentionally helping another to engage in an act of academic misconduct, or attempts thereof.

G. VIOLATION OF UNIVERSITY, COLLEGE, DEPARTMENTAL, PROGRAM, COURSE, OR FACULTY RULES

The violation of any University, College, Departmental, Program, Course, or Faculty Rules relating to academic matters that may lead to an unfair academic advantage by the student violating the rule(s).

Plagiarism

Plagiarism may take many forms, each of which is unacceptable, according to the standards of academic honesty as governed by the Virginia Tech Honor System. Any written or oral work you present as your own for this class should be completely your own--content, organization, language choices, visuals--unless you **orally** cite sources.

<u>Resources</u> - Plagiarism and Consequences

- O'Hair, Chapter 5
- Virginia Tech Library: http://www.lib.vt.edu/help/plagiarism.html
- University Honor System website: http://www.honorsystem.vt.edu/

<u>**Potential Plagiarism Problems**</u> -- The following examples--adapted from a list by Dr. Rachel Holloway, Vice Provost for Undergraduate Academic Affairs--illustrate areas in which students might make ethical errors with their oral or written presentations. This list identifies the most frequent of such dishonest behaviors:

1. Representation of someone else's words or ideas without acknowledgment of the original source -- This includes exact quotation, paraphrase of ideas, duplication of organizational design, recounting of narratives, or other content, without appropriate attribution. A student may avoid plagiarism by citing the source of the materials in the speech performance. Simply including the sources on a bibliography without clear citation in the speech or paper misrepresents the origin of the ideas/materials to the immediate audience and would constitute plagiarism. Carefully document your sources!

2. Representation of visual or graphic materials as one's own work when they are duplicated from some other source or created with the help of another individual --The Honor System bans "work for hire" or "purchased work." This does not mean that you are forbidden to use technology to for visual aids. Give appropriate credit by orally citing sources.

3. Use of "file" speeches or papers --Your presentations are to be the product of your original research, thought, and composition. Simply rephrasing or reordering the ideas, organization, supporting materials, or any other element of a presentation from someone else's preparation and materials does not meet the requirements of original work and is an honor code violation. Extemporaneous delivery of a stolen or borrowed speech does not exempt a student from plagiarism charges.

4. Use of a misleading bibliography to "document" your speech -- A bibliography must include only the materials used in the development of the presentation. Inclusion of materials that were not used for analysis or incorporated into a presentation constitutes a violation of the Honor Code.

Course Basics, Part VI -- Calendar

In order to achieve effective learning with efficient use of time, students have a high level of personal responsibility in this course. That responsibility (1) allows you great autonomy with your time online and (2) minimizes the number of times you actually have to be in the classroom.

Creating your calendar --

For your convenience, a tentative calendar is provided with dates for this semester.

1. Number the M-W-F classes (1-43) this semester. We'll be referring to these class numbers across the semester.
2. Check the Calendar provided on the Canvas site, and indicate in each of your 43 class blocks either "I" (dates when you'll be IN the classroom) or "O" (dates when your class work is ONLINE).
3. Note online quiz dates -- "Q"; 5 major speech dates -- "S"; and final exam (determined according to Timetable) -- "E"
4. Add any other dates now or as we move through the semester. Some online work may be distributed across the week so that you'll have more time to complete certain assignments.

Name _____

Maroon or Orange? _____

Public Speaking Dates &Assignments   Spring 2018

Class Meetings – 27 total days in the classroom --
    * Last classes before Spring break

Info Days-- Information provided to clarify assignments for the unit. Students should have read related chapters and reviewed info in *Course Guide* before that class meeting and should bring topic ideas to class or submit online, based on Instructor's request.

Prep Days-- Oranges or Maroons meet to share outlines, problem-solve, and practice strategies.

Resources -- Additional resources provided online, such as library information and samples speeches. Students should refer to these resources as they develop their speeches.

Midterm—Refers to an online assessment of your perceptions of and progress in this class; NOT an actual exam.

Final Exam—Cumulative online exam, including information from textbook readings, Units I-V.

Public Speaking Dates &Assignments   Spring 2018

I=In the classroom (*italics--all in*) O=Online class **Bold**=Assignment due

Class		Maroon due dates	Orange due dates
1	W Jan 17	*I - Intro to course*	*I - Intro to course*
2	F 19	*I - Info Day Unit I-Reading;* **PRPSA due**	*I - Info Day Unit I-Reading;* **PRPSA due**
3	M 22	*I - Prep Day;* **Outline due; REAL PS 1 due**	O - Reading Unit I
4	W 24	O - **Quiz I** & Speech Rehearsal	*I - Prep Day;* **Outline due; REAL PS 1 due**
5	F 26	*I - **Speech 1 & Outline due***	O – **Quiz I**
6	M 29	*I - **Speech 1 & Outline due***	O – Speech Rehearsal
7	W 31	O - Reading Unit II	*I - **Speech 1 & Outline due***
8	F Feb 2	O - **Quiz II**	*I - **Speech 1 & Outline due***
9	M 5	*I - Info Day A Unit II;* **REAL PS 2 due**	*I - Info Day A Unit II;* **REAL PS 2 due**
10	W 7	*I – Info Day B Unit II*	*I – Info Day B Unit II*
11	F 9	*I - Prep Day-* **Outline & Bib due**	O – Reading Unit II; **Quiz II**
12	M 12	O - Speech Research & Rehearsal	*I - Prep Day -* **Outline & Bib due**
13	W 14	*I - **Speech 2 Outline & Bib due***	O – Speech Prep
14	F 16	*I - **Speech 2 Outline & Bib due***	O – Speech Prep
15	M 19	*I - **Speech 2 Outline & Bib due***	O – Speech Rehearsal
16	W 21	O - Reading Unit III	*I - **Speech 2 Outline & Bib due***
17	F 23	O - Speech Research Unit III	*I - **Speech 2 Outline & Bib due***
18	M 26	O - **Quiz Unit III**	*I - **Speech 2 Outline & Bib due***
19	W 28	*I - Info Day Unit III;* **REAL PS 3; Midterm due**	*I - Info Day Unit III;* **REAL PS 3; Midterm due**
20	F Mar 2 *	*I- Prep Day Speech 3;* **Outline/bib, Audience due**	O - Reading Unit III; **Quiz III**
		***SPRING BREAK**	***SPRING BREAK**
21	M 12	O - Speech Rehearsal	*I - Prep Day Speech 3;* **Outline/bib, Audience due**
22	W 14	*I - **Speech 3; Final Outline/ Bib, audience due***	O – Speech Prep
23	F 16	*I - **Speech 3; Final Outline/ Bib, audience due***	O – Speech Research
24	M 19	*I - **Speech 3; Final Outline/ Bib, audience due***	O – Speech Rehearsal
25	W 21	O - Reading Unit IV	*I - **Speech 3; Final Outline/ Bib, audience due***
26	F 23	O - Speech Research Unit IV	*I - **Speech 3; Final Outline/ Bib, audience due***
27	M 26	O - **Quiz IV**	*I - **Speech 3; Final Outline/ Bib, audience due***
28	W 28	*I – Info Day Unit IV;* **REAL PS 4 due**	*I - Info Day Unit IV;* **REAL PS 4 due**
29	F 30	*I – Prep Day;* **Outline, bib, context due**	O –Reading Unit IV; **Quiz IV**
30	M Apr 2	O - Speech Prep/Rehearsal	*I - Prep Day;* **Outline, bib, context due**
31	W 4	*I - **Speech 4; Final Outline/bib, etc. due***	O – Speech Prep
32	F 6	*I - **Speech 4; Final Outline/bib, etc. due***	O - Speech Prep
33	M 9	*I - **Speech 4; Final Outline/bib, etc. due***	O - Speech Prep
34	W 11	*I-**Speech 4; Final Outline, etc. due**; Review Sp5*	O - Speech Prep/Rehearsal
35	F 13	O - Reading Unit V	*I - **Speech 4; Final Outline/bib, etc. due***
36	M 16	O - Unit V	*I - **Speech 4; Final Outline/bib, etc. due***
37	W 18	O - Speech Prep	*I - **Speech 4; Final Outline/bib, etc. due***
38	F 20	O - **Quiz V**	*I - **Speech 4; Final Outline, etc. due**; Review Sp5*
39	M 23	*I - Info Day Unit V*	*I - Info Day Unit V;* **Quiz V**
40	W 25	*I - Prep Day Unit 5;* **REAL PS 5 due**	*I - Prep Day Unit 5;* **REAL PS 5 due**
41	F 27	*I - **Group Speeches; Final outline/bib due***	*I - **Group Speeches; Final outline/bib due***
42	M 30	*I - **Group Speeches; Final outline/bib due***	*I - **Group Speeches; Final outline/bib due***
43	W May 2	*I - **Reflection assignment; PRPSA due***	*I - **Reflection assignment; PRPSA due***
Final Exam		**Online Exam on scheduled exam day**	**Online Exam on scheduled exam day**

Class Meetings -- 27 total days in the classroom --
  * Last class before Spring break

Info Days-- Information provided to clarify assignments for the unit. Students should have read related chapters and reviewed info in *Course Guide* before that class meeting and should bring topic ideas to class or submit online, based on Instructor's request.

Prep Days-- Oranges or Maroons meet to share outlines, problem-solve, and practice strategies.

Midterm—Refers to an online assessment of your perceptions of and progress in this class; NOT an actual exam.

Final Exam—Cumulative online exam, including information from textbook readings, Units I-V.

Unit I -- Narrative Speech

1. Reading	*Course Guide* -- Intro materials Ch. 1-4 – Becoming a Public Speaker, Managing Anxiety, Listening Ch. 13 – Outlining Ch. 18 – Vocal delivery Presentation speeches Sample speeches – p. 33 O'Hair and Canvas site
2. Quiz	*Course Guide, Chapters 1-4, 13, 18, and sample speeches*
3. Participation	Online and in-class activities; PRPSA Research participation; REAL PS 1
4. Speech	Narration

REAL PS 1 -- Narration

     As an introduction to REAL PS, we'll begin our exploration of the four components that underscore every speaking experience:

     Research -- Generating detail from personal experience

     Ethics -- Personal credibility; plagiarism in PS

     Analysis -- Consideration of personal confidence and competence

     Language/**L**istening -- Listening to fellow speakers; open-mindedness -- Chapter 3

     For more information about the REAL PS segments of this course, see the introductory information in this *Course Guide* or check Canvas. REAL PS topics are designed to enhance your understanding of the course concepts.

What's Your Story?

     So that you can begin to think about narration let your instructor know something about your background and goals, please respond to the following questions. Your instructor will collect this information either in class or online.

1. What's your personal history with public speaking?

2. Aside from meeting a requirement, why are you taking this course?

3. What do you expect to learn in this course that you don't already know about public speaking?

4. How do you expect to use improved PS skills in your other classes or in your career?

Note: Take survey online – PRPSA – Bring hard copy and score to next class.

Speech 1 -- Narrative Speech

Your first formal speaking assignment is one most familiar to you already. You will be telling a personal story to the class.

Many speakers use stories to illustrate main ideas. Those stories may be entertaining, informational, or inspirational. Often, your professors will tell personal stories to relate the lecture content to you as students. As you consider this narrative speech assignment, think of this speech as an opportunity to tell your classmates more about yourself and to get to know each other.

Build a speech around a true event that was meaningful in your life. Narrow your speech to a specific event, so that your speech will be effective and easy to prepare. The speech should include autobiographical significance; that is, you should explain why the incident is significant to you in some way. Usually speakers include this explanation in the introduction or conclusion.

This speech establishes your credibility for upcoming speeches and allows you to test your speaking ability. Since no outside research is required for this speech, you'll be able to focus on chronological organization and delivery. You might even have fun with this presentation!

As an audience member, you'll also have the opportunity to build (1) your skills as an evaluator and (2) a better understanding of your classmates.

Guidelines for Speech 1

Complexity	Level 1 -- See chart of speeches, page 4
Type	Narrative; extemporaneous
Topic choice/focus	Personal story of true event with autobiographical significance Limited in scope
Audience	Classmates; analysis -- age
Purpose	Inform; socialize
Credibility	Personal integrity; sincerity; connection with audience
Support	<ul><li>Illustration, narrative</li><li>Use of specific and vivid detail</li><li>Includes autobiographical significance</li></ul>
Organization	Chronological order
Voice & language	Vocal clarity and volume
Physical behaviors	Eye contact; posture; use of speaking notes; facial expression to match mood
Presentation aids	Object; personal appearance
Time	2 ½ - 4 ½ minutes
Note card	1-2 4x6 cards -- white, with large lettering of key words-- no sentences While you might know this story well, this speech provides a good opportunity to practice using a note card. The card will also help to build your confidence because it provides a back-up for you. The size of the card is best for speech notes because it is roomier than the smaller cards, so you need fewer and can have more white space. You want to be able to glance briefly at the card and find a word easily. Your instructor will collect your note card after your speech.

Topic Possibilities -- Narrative speech

As you consider your first speech, be sure to review the related materials in O'Hair. The sample speech at the end of Chapter 2 is more of an overview than a narrative, but it certainly includes some narrative components. The speech you'll be giving will focus more on one event in your life -- NOT a "highlights of me" kind of speech.

Meaning -- Because this assignment also requires some statement of autobiographical significance, you should consider an event that generated emotion and had some lasting meaning for you; maybe it was startling, embarrassing, sad, inspirational, tragic, or funny. Something about this even caused you to remember it and maybe even learn from it. Be careful that the emotion is manageable as you recall it in your speech. Avoid describing severe tragedy or pain because you may be overcome with those emotions during the speech.

Scope -- You might be tempted to focus on major events, but those events are impossible to explain in detail in the limited amount of time for this speech. Choose something that the listeners can identify with -- a story about your family, your roommate, your first day at a new job, one afternoon in a foreign country, one game of golf, one time when you were lost, etc. For example, you can't tell the story of your whole trip to Spain, but you can tell about the day your backpack was stolen while you were there.

Recent event -- If you choose an event that has happened fairly recently, you'll be better able to recall the specific details necessary to paint a picture of the scene for listeners.

Connecting, not lecturing -- When you explain the autobiographical significance to your listeners, be sure that you don't lecture them or expect them to have the same response to your story. Avoid, "The moral of this story is. . ." Rather, you should use the story to share something unique about yourself with them. Focus on the event's impact in your life.

Generating topic ideas -- Brainstorm a list of at least ten possibilities. Write as fast as you can; don't judge each possibility. Try responding to these prompts --
- An adventure -- with a roommate? Best friend? Sibling?
- First days -- at VT? In a new dorm? In a new workplace? In a new home? Etc.
- Family rituals -- this year's holidays? An outdoor adventure? A vacation?
- Pet stories? Adoption? Loss? Birth?
- Favorite places? Why? What happened there?
- Pranks?

Once you respond to some of these possibilities, add more ideas. Talk to your roommate or a family member to explore some ideas.

Selecting a topic -- Narrow the list of possibilities to 3, and match those against the assignment guidelines. Can you create a vivid picture for your listeners and develop a story line in just a few minutes? Can you find an object to enhance your speech as a presentation aid? Choose the best topic to develop into a speech.

Generating details about the topic -- Don't write out the story. Just make a list of names and descriptions that come to mind as you recall the story. Who was there? What sensory details come to mind about the experience? (What did you smell, taste, touch, hear, see?) As you put the story together, you'll invite your listeners to share the event with you -- pull them in by providing rich detail.

Speech preparation and delivery:

Successful presentations will necessitate the completion of the following steps:

- **Invention**
  - o Choose an appropriate topic (previous page)
  - o Determine audience needs
  - o Generate supporting detail
- **Arrangement**
  - o Organize your narrative into a clear chronological structure
  - o Formulate introduction, transitions, and conclusion
- **Style**
  - o Consider the language you'll use to connect with the audience
  - o Sensory detail helps the listeners to share the experience with you.
- **Memory and Delivery**
  - o Design and create a presentation aid – object (See O'Hair, Chapter 20)
  - o Rehearse
  - o Present, using 1-2 (maximum) 4x6 cards

Related writing

- Presentation plan
- Critiques of peers' speeches

Preston MAP Strategy: M.A.P. to Successful Presentations

Headed to an important interview? Visiting prospective graduate schools? Traveling to an away football game? Taking a weekend road trip?

Even for an impromptu trip, you grab a map and plot your course before you get too far along the way to a place you haven't visited before. You can make the trip without the map, but your efforts would not be predictable and could result in a disaster!

When you plan an oral presentation, you must also begin with a MAP if you want to heighten your chances for success. By making three decisions early in the process, you will reach your destination on time, ready to make an effective presentation.

1. Message? What message do you want to deliver? In one sentence or phrase, what is the narrowed topic of your speech or report? What should someone understand after you've finished that he or she didn't understand before? This statement of message may evolve into the thesis of your presentation.

2. Audience? What specific group of people will receive your message? Once you determine the identity of this group, you'll want to do an audience analysis to determine what they already know about your message, why they care about it, what they need from the situation you're discussing, etc. Since your presentations will be geared for students or professionals in specific circumstances, avoid those boring speeches to the "general public."

3. Purpose? What do you want to accomplish with your presentation? Why do you want to tell your audience about the topic you've chosen? Do you want to entertain them? inform them? This general purpose will be refined later to a more specific purpose.

You might use brainstorming or freewriting to make these decisions; you might even begin with the purpose: to inform). However, once you've made these three decisions, you'll be able to eliminate any ideas that don't fit your M.A.P. and create a logical route to an effective presentation.

Presentation Plan/ KEYWORD Outline
> **Use this template as a model for your own typed outline** -- keyword, not sentence outline.
> Your instructor will evaluate this presentation plan as part of the "message preparation" for this speech.

MAP -- Message: Audience: **P**urpose: To inform/socialize

Introduction
> Attention-getting strategy:
> Motivate the audience -- Relevance
> Thesis: *(Suggest the focus and tone of the story. Don't give away any surprises.)*

Transition to first main point:

I. _____ *(Write first main point here.)*
> Include the **rising action** in this section – set the scene; introduce the conflict/challenge and the characters.
> A.
> > 1.
> > 2.
> B.
> > 1.
> > 2.

Transition – Write out your transition statement

II. _____ *(Second main point)*
> Further develop the plot with specific details and include the **climax** in this section.
> A.
> > 1.
> > 2.
> B.
> > 1.
> > 2.

Transition - Write out your transition statement

III. _____ *(Third main point)*
> Explain the **falling action or resolution** in this section.
> A.
> > 1.
> > 2.
> B.
> > 1.
> > 2.

Transition to conclusion - Write out your transition statement
Conclusion:
> A. Restate thesis
> B. Memorable thought/Psychological Closure

Notes:
- *Your outline might have 3 or 4 main points. While they should be balanced, they may not be equal in emphasis. Information leading to the climax might take more development than information after the climax.*
- *Required paperwork for speeches will usually count as 10% of the speech grade.*

Counting Down -- Rehearsing and Presenting

During the days before your speech

1. Finalize presentation plan after double-checking assignment requirements and the critique forms. Review the checklist at the end of Chapter 2, O'Hair.
2. Prepare note card (keywords only, large writing, plenty of white space) and presentation aid
3. Rehearse with note card (in non-dominant hand) and presentation aid –
   - See O'Hair, Chapter 2, "Practice Delivering the Speech"
   - Display the object only when appropriate; hold it at shoulder-height for at least 20-30 seconds. See O'Hair, Chap. 20 – "Incorporating Presentation Aids into Your Speech"
   - Time your rehearsal
   Caution: Rehearse, but stop short of memorizing your speech. Maintain a conversational style.
4. Decide on your "look" for the speech (See note below about appearance.)

Appearance choices -- No hats, no hats, no hats, no hats, no hats, no hats!

1. Your choice of dress depends on the identity of your audience. Generally, you should dress in a slightly more formal way than your audience. When you present a story to your classmates, you should look like a college student to enhance your connection with your audience. If you wear your prom dress or your interview suit, that connection with your audience will be lessened. Of course, if you are returning to your high school to discuss interview skills with high school seniors, then your interview suit is appropriate.
2. Plan your appearance ahead of time.
3. Choose clothes/accessories that are comfortable and won't distract you (or the audience) with slipping zippers, bare stomachs, or annoying jangling.
4. Whatever you choose, be sure that your clothes are clean and neat.

Night before your speech

1. Final rehearsal
2. Create a "mental movie" of your successful presentation. Focus on the success and sense of sharing you'll have with other students in the class. Everyone is at least a little nervous, and everyone in the class is hoping that speeches are interesting and pleasant.
3. Be sure that your paperwork is ready for the next day. Don't forget the critique forms!
4. Get a good night's sleep so that you'll be refreshed and alert for the next day's presentation.

Morning of your speech

1. Eat!
2. Get to class a little early so that you're not racing and flustered.
3. Try square breathing while you're waiting for your turn to speak. Focus fully on others' speeches, especially those for whom you're writing critiques.

Your turn to present

1. Stand in front of the room, pause, look at other students, and smile (if appropriate)
2. Pause before beginning and speak slowly. The audience is getting used to your voice and your manner. You can increase your pace as the speech moves on and the audience is engaged.
3. After the last line of your conclusion, avoid saying "that's it" or some other line that distracts from or minimizes your speech. Pause and return to your seat.

Speech Critiques -- Providing and Receiving Feedback

Value of Critiques. Peer critiques are useful to a speaker and also to the reviewer.

For Speakers -- Peer feedback on developmental stages of a speech and/or on the final speech can be extremely helpful. When we consider our own work, we often see what we <u>meant</u> to convey in an outline, PowerPoint, or final speech, rather than what we actually conveyed. Peer reviewers can ask questions and point out gaps in logic or sequence. If several peers review your work, you will gain insight from the audience perspective and many suggestions for improvement.

For Reviewers -- Reviewers not only earn participation points, but they also gain practice with analysis, problem-solving, and tactful expression of ideas – certainly useful skills for the classroom and the career.

Offering Feedback. Students often say that they are not qualified to write critiques, they don't want to criticize their friends, and they're uncomfortable making notes about other students' speeches. Of course, a peer critique DOES reflect the perceptions of one person, so a speaker will weigh those comments and select the most useful ones help direct him or her in a subsequent speech.

As you build your listening and analysis skills, you'll learn to write good critiques. You'll get better and better at finding the words to effectively, honestly, AND tactfully characterize the strengths and weaknesses in a presentation. Make comments that will help the presenter maintain the effective aspects of speaking and improve the weak aspects. Avoid being vicious or syrupy sweet. Either extreme is useless to the speaker. Be constructive!

Completing Critiques of Speeches

- Before the presentation, familiarize yourself with the form to be used for that assignment. This will allow you to fill out a form easily and quickly during someone's speech.
- During the assigned speech, please be discreet while writing. You certainly don't want to distract the speaker! Keep your eyes on the speaker as much as possible so that you can accurately analyze the speaker's movement, eye contact, and other aspects of the speech.
- You may need to finish the form between other speeches, before you leave at the end of the class period, or even during other speeches. Again, discretion please! Add as much detail as possible.
- In the case of absence, peer critiques cannot be made up at a later date. *Missed critiques will result in zero participation points.*

Receiving Feedback. You'll be getting notes on your speeches from your instructor and your peers.

Instructor feedback -- You will be asked to submit forms for instructor feedback on your speaking. In return, you will receive comments about the strengths of your work and the areas needing improvement. Please take the time to review these comments and to request clarification if a comment is not clear.

Peer feedback – Accept the comments in the spirit in which they were given. You classmates are not speech experts, but they are quite experienced as audience members. They are simply sharing their perceptions of your speech and their suggestions for improvement. Be grateful for their honesty and their encouragement.

Using Feedback for Improvement. As the speaker, you should consider any themes that seem to occur in multiple critiques. These are the areas that were evident to several people in your audience, and they deserve attention as you prepare your next speech. Develop the habit of reviewing these forms whenever you begin developing a subsequent speech.

Speech Critique Components. Following is a list of general competencies that will be considered for each oral presentation. Your instructor will discuss each of these categories with you so that you know how you will be evaluated and how to evaluate others. This list is adapted with permission from the "Competent Speaker" Speech Evaluation Form by Sherwyn Morreale, Michael Moore, Donna Surges-Tatum, and Linda Webster (2ⁿᵈ edition, 2007). "The Competent Speaker" was developed by the National Communication Association (formerly Speech Communication Association) Committee for Assessment and Testing and representatives from 12 academic institutions.

Part I. Message Preparation
1. Topic and Connection with Audience
Selection and narrowing of a topic appropriate for audience and occasion.
2. Thesis/Specific Purpose
Clarification of the thesis and/or specific purpose in a manner appropriate for the audience and occasion.
3. Support
a. Supporting material -- use of examples, details, research, and/or argument, appropriate for the audience and occasion.
b. Presentation aids -- design of visual and/or audio support to enhance the speech, including the use of PowerPoint, objects, handouts, etc.
4. Organization
Use of an organizational pattern appropriate to topic, audience, occasion & purpose.
- Introduction with attention-getter, connection with audience, preview or focus statements
- Organization enhanced with transitions
- Conclusion with impact

Part II. Message Delivery
5. Language (Choice of language is part of "message preparation"; use of language is part of "message delivery.")
Use of language appropriate to the audience, occasion & purpose
6. Vocal Variety
Use of vocal variety in rate, pitch & intensity to heighten and maintain interest
7. Vocal Accuracy (Intelligibility)
Use of accurate pronunciation, grammar, & articulation
8. Physical Behaviors -- Use of movement & gestures that support the message, including eye contact; facial expression; sincerity, warmth, enthusiasm, natural gesture, posture, movement; appropriate use of notes and presentation aids; and appropriate appearance

Name _____

Instructor Summary of Feedback -- Narrative Speech

      Please attach this form to your presentation plan; the critique for instructor's use is on the back of this page. The outline must be available to your instructor before you can give your speech.

      After your speech, your instructor will review his or her notes on a critique form and any forms that your peers completed about your speech. Your instructor might use ✓ , ✓ + or ✓ - on some of the lines below to show your general accomplishment in the areas listed. When the papers are returned to you, please use this form along with the instructor critique form to review your feedback. If there's something you don't understand, be sure to ask about it.

Message Preparation   (50%) _____

             Outline   (10%) _____

Message Delivery   (40%)_____

Speech Grade   _____

<u>Notes – Overall strengths and suggestions for next speech</u>:

Narrative -- Critique Form Speaker _____

Missing, Ineffective, Satisfactory, Good, Excellent *Notes*

Competencies	*Part I: Message Preparation -- Appropriate for speaker, topic, audience, occasion, and purpose*	M	I	S	G	E
Topic	* Chooses and narrows a topic					
	Meets general purpose – to inform					
Support/ Organization	* Uses narrative organization pattern (Rising action—climax—falling action)					
	Intro – Uses attention-getter; identifies topic & purpose; establishes relevance; transitions to 1ˢᵗ main point					
	Body -- Provides appropriate supporting material with **vivid and specific details**					
	* Chronological order with **transitions**					
	Conclusion -- Restatement of thesis; memorable thought					
	Part I: Overall					
	Part II Energetic Message Delivery – Appropriate for audience, occasion, and purpose	M	I	S	G	E
Language	Uses appropriate language for the designated audience					
Voice	* **Variety --** Uses vocal variety in volume, rate, pitch & intensity to heighten and maintain interest.					
	Accuracy -- Uses pronunciation, grammar, & articulation; minimizes filler words					
Physical Behaviors	**Appearance and manner --** Stands with shoulders straight, head up, assertive stance; dressed appropriately					
	Movement and gestures – Uses movement and gestures effectively					
	Facial expression and eye contact -- Uses facial expressiveness and eye contact to support the message and engage with listeners					
	* **Presentation aid --** Effectively presents object to support message					
	Note cards – Appropriately designed notecards; Effectively uses note cards to support speech					
Time?	*Part II: Overall*					

*** Focal points for this speech –** addressed in reading and homework*

Notes:

Narrative -- Critique Form　　　　　　　　　　**Speaker** _____

Competencies	Part I: Message Preparation -- Appropriate for speaker, topic, audience, occasion, and purpose	M	I	S	G	E
Topic	* Chooses and narrows a topic					
	Meets general purpose – to inform					
Support/ Organization	* Uses narrative organization pattern (Rising action—climax—falling action)					
	Intro – Uses attention-getter; identifies topic & purpose; establishes relevance; transitions to 1ˢ main point					
	Body -- Provides appropriate supporting material with **vivid and specific details**					
	* Chronological order with **transitions**					
	Conclusion -- Restatement of thesis; memorable thought					
	Part I: Overall					
	Part II Energetic Message Delivery – Appropriate for audience, occasion, and purpose	M	I	S	G	E
Language	Uses appropriate language for the designated audience					
Voice	* **Variety** -- Uses vocal variety in volume, rate, pitch & intensity to heighten and maintain interest.					
	Accuracy -- Uses pronunciation, grammar, & articulation; minimizes filler words					
Physical Behaviors	**Appearance and manner** -- Stands with shoulders straight, head up, assertive stance; dressed appropriately					
	Movement and gestures – Uses movement and gestures effectively					
	Facial expression and eye contact -- Uses facial expressiveness and eye contact to support the message and engage with listeners					
	* **Presentation aid --** Effectively presents object to support message					
	Note cards – Appropriately designed notecards; Effectively uses note cards to support speech					
Time?	*Part II: Overall*					

The column headers at top read: Missing, Ineffective, Satisfactory, Good, Excellent　*Notes*

* Focal points for this speech – addressed in reading and homework

Notes:
Most effective aspects of speech?

Suggestions for improvement?　　　　　　**Critiqued by?** _____

Narrative -- Critique Form **Speaker _______________**

Missing, **I**neffective, **S**atisfactory, **G**ood, **E**xcellent *Notes*

Competencies	***Part I: Message Preparation -- Appropriate for speaker, topic, audience, occasion, and purpose***	**M**	**I**	**S**	**G**	**E**
Topic	* Chooses and narrows a topic					
	Meets general purpose – to inform					
Support/ Organization	* Uses narrative organization pattern (Rising action—climax—falling action)					
	Intro – Uses attention-getter; identifies topic & purpose; establishes relevance; transitions to 1st main point					
	Body -- Provides appropriate supporting material with **vivid and specific details**					
	* Chronological order with **transitions**					
	Conclusion -- Restatement of thesis; memorable thought					
	Part I: Overall					
	Part II <u>Energetic</u> Message Delivery – Appropriate for audience, occasion, and purpose	**M**	**I**	**S**	**G**	**E**
Language	Uses appropriate language for the designated audience					
Voice	* **Variety** -- Uses vocal variety in volume, rate, pitch & intensity to heighten and maintain interest.					
	Accuracy -- Uses pronunciation, grammar, & articulation; minimizes filler words					
Physical Behaviors	**Appearance and manner** -- Stands with shoulders straight, head up, assertive stance; dressed appropriately					
	Movement and gestures – Uses movement and gestures effectively					
	Facial expression and eye contact -- Uses facial expressiveness and eye contact to support the message and engage with listeners					
	* **Presentation aid --** Effectively presents object to support message					
	Note cards – Appropriately designed notecards; Effectively uses note cards to support speech					
Time?	***Part II: Overall***					

*** Focal points for this speech –** *addressed in reading and homework*

Notes:

Most effective aspects of speech?

Suggestions for improvement? **Critiqued by? ____________________**

Narrative -- Critique Form **Speaker** ______________

Missing, Ineffective, Satisfactory, Good, Excellent *Notes*

Competencies	*Part I: Message Preparation -- Appropriate for speaker, topic, audience, occasion, and purpose*	M	I	S	G	E
Topic	* Chooses and narrows a topic					
	Meets general purpose – to inform					
Support/ Organization	* Uses narrative organization pattern (Rising action—climax—falling action)					
	Intro – Uses attention-getter; identifies topic & purpose; establishes relevance; transitions to 1st main point					
	Body -- Provides appropriate supporting material with **vivid and specific details**					
	* Chronological order with **transitions**					
	Conclusion -- Restatement of thesis; memorable thought					
	Part I: Overall					
	Part II <u>Energetic</u> Message Delivery – Appropriate for audience, occasion, and purpose	**M**	**I**	**S**	**G**	**E**
Language	Uses appropriate language for the designated audience					
Voice	* **Variety** -- Uses vocal variety in volume, rate, pitch & intensity to heighten and maintain interest.					
	Accuracy -- Uses pronunciation, grammar, & articulation; minimizes filler words					
Physical Behaviors	**Appearance and manner** -- Stands with shoulders straight, head up, assertive stance; dressed appropriately					
	Movement and gestures – Uses movement and gestures effectively					
	Facial expression and eye contact -- Uses facial expressiveness and eye contact to support the message and engage with listeners					
	* **Presentation aid --** Effectively presents object to support message					
	Note cards – Appropriately designed notecards; Effectively uses note cards to support speech					
Time?	***Part II: Overall***					

*** Focal points for this speech** – *addressed in reading and homework*

Notes:
Most effective aspects of speech?

Suggestions for improvement? **Critiqued by?** ________________

Narrative -- Critique Form

Speaker _____

Competencies	**Part I: Message Preparation -- Appropriate for speaker, topic, audience, occasion, and purpose**	M	I	S	G	E	
Topic	* Chooses and narrows a topic						
	Meets general purpose – to inform						
Support/ Organization	* Uses narrative organization pattern (Rising action—climax—falling action)						
	Intro – Uses attention-getter; identifies topic & purpose; establishes relevance; transitions to 1ˢᵗ main point						
	Body -- Provides appropriate supporting material with **vivid and specific details**						
	* Chronological order with **transitions**						
	Conclusion -- Restatement of thesis; memorable thought						
	Part I: Overall						
	Part II _Energetic_ Message Delivery – Appropriate for audience, occasion, and purpose	M	I	S	G	E	
Language	Uses appropriate language for the designated audience						
Voice	* **Variety** -- Uses vocal variety in volume, rate, pitch & intensity to heighten and maintain interest.						
	Accuracy -- Uses pronunciation, grammar, & articulation; minimizes filler words						
Physical Behaviors	**Appearance and manner** -- Stands with shoulders straight, head up, assertive stance; dressed appropriately						
	Movement and gestures – Uses movement and gestures effectively						
	Facial expression and eye contact -- Uses facial expressiveness and eye contact to support the message and engage with listeners						
	* **Presentation aid** -- Effectively presents object to support message						
	Note cards – Appropriately designed notecards; Effectively uses note cards to support speech						
Time?	*Part II: Overall*						

Missing, Ineffective, Satisfactory, Good, Excellent   *Notes*

* *Focal points for this speech –* addressed in reading and homework

Notes:
Most effective aspects of speech?

Suggestions for improvement?   **Critiqued by?** _____

Steps to Self-Assessment and Improvement

Fill in the following chart each time you get your speech critique back. When your speech folder is returned to you, summarize the instructor comments in the designated column below. Find sections in O'Hair that relate to those comments, and then determine what steps you'll need to take to conquer those speaking issues before the next speech is due. Your instructor may ask that you staple this page in your folder so that you both can refer to it easily.

Assignment	Instructor comments (Summarize instructor notes -- strengths, suggestions.)	Related sections in O'Hair	Improvement plan (Identify your plan to improve before the next speech.)
Narrative speech			
Concept speech			
Progress Report speech			
Issue Analysis speech			

Print Name_____

Managing Your Course Responsibilities

During the first week of class, you created a calendar of due dates. The structure of the course offers you lots of discretion about using your time because you don't have to be in class 3 hours each week. The course runs on a clear and precise schedule, though, so you have to pay careful attention to in-class dates and online assignment dates. Consider that attention a kind of trade-off for all of the days you don't have to be in the classroom!

Preparing for class -- You often have assignments that will help you to prepare a speech, such as considerations of speech topics, audience analysis, or outlines. These assignments will be checked in class, and you'll be awarded participation points for your efforts. Of course, these assignments are important so that you will have your speech prepared effectively. This preparation will lead to more successful speeches! If you come to class without the assignment, your instructor may accept the assignment one day later with the equivalent of a letter grade penalty.

Attending class -- Attendance in class is crucial. These class meetings are designed to support you as you develop a speech and to provide an environment in which you will be as comfortable as possible giving a speech. <u>Of course you need an audience for your speeches, and you need to BE an audience for your classmates.</u> You'll also have the opportunity to learn from other speakers and to earn participation points by providing feedback for them.

Missing a speech -- Because of the number of speakers, there is no allowance for make-up speeches. *If you miss a speaking date, you'll receive a 0 for the speech and you'll fail the course. You must present all formal speeches in order to pass the class.*

Of course, if you are hospitalized or have some major crisis, your instructor will try to help you make a plan for your speech once your absence is documented through your Dean's Office. However, your instructor will NOT accept notes from your doctor or health center, email from your mom, or phone calls from your roommate as excuses for your absence. If you have a major **unforeseeable** difficulty that affects your attendance in **all** of your classes, you should take the documentation of your absence (such as a dated doctor's note indicating that you should stay out of class) to your Dean's Office. If your Dean's Office excuses you, your instructor will receive a notice to that effect.

Keeping up with online work -- Online quizzes, homework assignments, reports of personal apprehension or progress, and midterm assessments are designed to help you be more successful in the course. Even if you don't have to be in the classroom, "online" days are equally important. Staying on track requires great time management—the kind of time management that you'll need in other courses and in your career. If you need support, ask your instructor for strategies or attend one of the many workshops on campus offered through the Counseling Center or the Student Success Center.

Research Participation

As indicated in the REAL PS theme of this course, all speeches require some level of research. The narrative speech builds on fairly informal research -- personal recollections, supporting ideas from those who may have shared an experience with you. Subsequent speeches require personal recollections, library and/or online research. With collecting data or supporting material of some type, speakers can try to make points, but they would have no substance with which to prove their points.

Research includes not only the review of library resources, but also personal projects that are designed to study an issue and create related data. This kind of primary research is conducted on campuses and many types of workplaces -- such as survey research, engineering projects, biology experiments, studies of building materials, or testing computer programs.

To increase your familiarity with different types of research, you will participate in a research project with the Department of Communication at some point in the semester. To participate, you'll enroll online, and then you'll be contacted whenever a research opportunity is available. Total time for this participation should be approximately one hour.

Although the requirement is noted as part of Unit V in the syllabus, you simply need to complete this requirement at some point before the last week of the semester.

Enrollment -- Instructions for enrolling are found on Canvas. Enroll *now* so that you have lots of options for research participation; then you'll be able to participate in the research that is scheduled at a time convenient for you. Once you create an account, you will be notified of studies automatically, so you should create an account soon to be sure that you have choices.

These points could make a difference for you at the end of the semester if you end up with a borderline grade. However, waiting until the end of the semester will mean that you probably won't have any opportunities to still participate!

Participation -- Once you sign up for a research opportunity, arrive promptly so that you can participate. Researchers often bar admittance to late students.

Be sure that you don't miss an event for which you've registered. If you hold a spot and don't use it, you're preventing others from participating. Your instructor will explain the consequences for missing a research opportunity for which you have registered.

To create an account, go to https://vt-comm.sona-systems.com/Default.aspx?ReturnUrl=/

If you have questions about the research projects, please contact the Research Committee, Department of Communication (www.comm.vt.edu).

Note: If you need to explore an alternative to the research participation, please see the Appendix at the end of this *Course Guide*. If you choose one of the alternative assignments, you must submit this assignment before the end of Unit V.

Unit II -- Concept Speech

1. Reading	*Course Guide* – **Unit II** Ch. 7 & 8 -- Topic, Purpose, Support Ch. 10– Citing Sources Ch.11 -- Organization Ch. 14 -- Introductions Ch. 19 -- Delivery Sample Speeches--Canvas and p. 208 O'Hair *(Note-- Parts of Ch. 6, 12, 20, & 23 addressed in this unit but not on quiz.)*
2. Quiz	*Course Guide; Chapters 7, 8, 10, 11, 14, 19; p. 208; sample speeches*
3. Participation	REAL PS 2 Online and in-class activities Midterm assessment
4. Speech	Concept

REAL PS 2 -- Concept Speech (Definition)

Research -- Choosing authoritative sources
Ethics -- Informing audience of non-experts
Analysis -- Analysis of audience and speech setting
Language/Listening -- Language for non-experts

Academic and professional speakers are often asked to define new concepts or redefine misunderstood concepts. Again, they use research, ethics, analysis, language, and listening as they develop and present their speeches. While you work on your speech, you'll be considering these components as part of REAL PS 2.

Concept Speech (Definition)

Your next formal speaking activity is to develop a speech defining a concept related to your major or perhaps higher education in general. In your narrative speech, you told a story about yourself. Details for that story came from your personal experience, and the story fell nicely into a chronological structure. However, most of your future speaking experiences will be much more complex than that. You will have to develop content from various resources and then formulate a logical, concise explanation of your material. Your clients, coworkers, and employers will value your ability to deliver succinct, clear presentations.

As college students, you have started to develop expertise in specific areas of study. But, could you take what you have learned and explain it to a newcomer with the same clarity and organization as your professors demonstrate? Your goal is to select a concept related to your major or to campus life that has sparked your interest and explain it to a group of students in an introductory course.

As you develop the speech, think about what your audience would need to know to grasp the concept. What would be the most effective way to explain it? What analogy will enhance understanding? What sources will be most useful? Remember, even though you are the expert on the topic, you will still need to use credible sources and establish the authenticity of your information by citing outside sources to back up your ideas.

What would be the best way to structure the speech so the audience could easily follow your train of thought? Develop main points that you will be able to logically link through transitions. Your speech should have a well organized body, a strong introduction and conclusion, and effective transitions.

Guidelines for Speech 2

Complexity	Level 2 -- includes level 1
Type	Concept; extemporaneous
Topic choice/focus	Concept or program related to higher ed or major
Audience	Students in an intro class in your major
Purpose	Inform
Credibility	Personal expertise as student; choice of valid and appropriate sources
Support	<ul><li>Definition, analogy, example</li><li>Minimum of 2 sources</li><li>Source citation: written bibliography **and** oral citation</li></ul> *Note: Insufficient oral citation will result in point deduction.*
Organization	Topical or spatial Emphasis on effective introductions and transitions
Voice & language	Vocal variety; Language appropriate for audience
Physical behaviors	Management of technology; variety of physical strategies
Presentation aid	Illustration; 1 image per slide -- 1-2 PowerPoint slides (plus spacer slides)
Time	3 ½ - 5 ½ minutes
Note cards	2-3 (maximum) 4x6 cards

Speech preparation and delivery

Successful presentations will necessitate the completion of the following steps:

- **Invention**
  - Choose an appropriate topic
  - Determine audience needs
  - Generate supporting detail from credible sources
- **Arrangement**
  - Organize into logical structure
  - Develop speech plan, including intro, transitions, and conclusions
- **Style**
  - Choose language appropriate for audience
  - Choose detail appropriate for audience
- **Memory and Delivery**
  - Prepare presentation aid (See types and strategies in O'Hair, Ch. 20)
  - Rehearse, using 4x6 note cards and slide
  - Present, using note cards and presentation aid

Related writing

- Presentation plan (with phrase or keyword outline) and bibliography in correct Chicago or APA form (see O'Hair Appendices)
- Critiques of peers' speeches

Topic Possibilities -- Concept Speech

Your choice of topic for your concept speech should be based on (1) your expertise with a concept in your major and (2) your further research about that concept. What concept could you explain to a lay audience -- people who have some interest in your major but who are not experts. (If you haven't taken any courses in your major, you could choose a concept from our Public Speaking textbook.) Brainstorm a list of at least ten topic possibilities. Choose a theory or term that will be intriguing -- perhaps the result of some new research. You might even ask an advisor or professor for some suggestions. Use the following prompts to get your list started:

1. List 2 or 3 concepts you learned in an intro course in your major.
2. What new research has developed in your field?
3. What new technology is being developed to support the professionals in your major?
4. List 2 or 3 advanced terms that you've tackled in an upper-level class.
5. List 2 or 3 ideas related to your major that caused YOU to be interested in the major.

Continue your list; flip through a textbook or an academic journal to get other ideas.

As you narrow your choices, keep in mind that you'll need a variety of types of sources, visuals (chart, graph or drawing) that will enhance understanding, and enthusiasm! Choose something that's interesting to you so that you can make it interesting to other people.

Next, narrow the focus. Consider the sample speech in Ch. 13 about mountain biking. Someone could write a whole book about spyware; what's one related term or concept that could make a good focus for a concept speech?

Research

For this speech, you should be able to use a textbook as one source. You might also interview a faculty member. Beyond that, you could use the library databases to find academic journals in your field. Check the correct documentation for these sources in Appendix B and Appendix C: **Journal article --**   **APA -- C #5**
Journal article from an online Database   **APA** -- C #6

Oral Citation of Sources -- Oral citation of sources is required so that you avoid plagiarizing information from other sources. Your listeners won't have a copy of your bibliography, so you need to let them know where you found your information. Citing sources also helps to enhance your credibility as a speaker because audiences will recognize not only that you've done your homework, but also that you chose a variety of types of valid resources.

The sources should be identified in your speech with enough information so that the listeners understand the source and the date. Chapter 8, O'Hair, includes examples of the types of citations you might include in your speech; chapter 10 explains how to cite sources orally.

Organization

Pay special attention to Chapters 11 and 12 as you consider the organization for this speech. You've already used chronological order; try topical, spatial, or cause-effect. O'Hair provides examples of each. Use the template of a presentation plan on the following page.

Presentation aid – Image Only

Design or select 1 or 2 images—photo, chart, graph—that will enhance your speech. Put the image or images on 1-2 PowerPoint slides; include a title for the slide at the top and any source information at the bottom (using small font for our own reference during the speech). The source is necessary only if you copied the image from another source; if you created the graph, you need not list yourself as the author. The image itself might have labels, but otherwise, the image should be non-text. No bullets! Such images are widely used in the workplace, but presenters often have had little practice with using them effectively.

Add spacer slides to separate the slides and allow you to go to a blank between images.

Practice incorporating the use of the slide into your speech. Refer to it; allow enough time for your audience to process the information. Although you need to look at the slide to be sure it's in focus, don't talk to the slide as you explain it to your audience. Be sure to face the audience as you explain the slide – even if you use a gesture to point to some component of the graph or chart.

Concept Speech -- Presentation Plan -- KEYWORD Outline

Use this template as a model and type your presentation plan to submit with your speech. Your instructor will evaluate your presentation plan as part of the "message preparation" for this speech grade. On the day of your speech, submit a typed copy of your presentation plan along with a critique sheet and the feedback summary page.

MAP -- Message: _____ Audience: _____ Purpose: To inform

Introduction

        Attention-getting strategy (p. 219):

        Topic and purpose (p. 224):

        Motivate the audience -- 1. Relevance to their interest, need? (p. 225)

                        2. Your credibility as a speaker on this topic? (p. 224)

        Preview of main ideas (p. 224):

Transition to first main point – Write out your transition statement

I. _____ *(List first main point here.)*

      A.

            1.

            2.

      B.

            1.

            2.

Transition – Write out your transition statement

II. _____ *(Second main point)*

      A.

            1.

            2.

      B.

            1.

            2.

Transition - Write out your transition statement

III. _____ *(Third main point)*

      A.

            1.

            2.

      B.

            1.

            2.

Transition - Write out your transition statement

Conclusion: See O'Hair, p. 227

Note: Bibliography will be short and can be placed on the same page as the outline.

Name _____

Instructor Summary of Feedback -- Concept Speech

      Please attach this form to your presentation plan; the critique for instructor's use is on the back of this page. The outline must be available to your instructor before you can give your speech.

      After your speech, your instructor will review his or her notes on a critique form and any forms that your peers completed about your speech. Your instructor might use ✓ , ✓ + or ✓ - on some of the lines below to show your general accomplishment in the areas listed. When the papers are returned to you, please use this form along with the instructor critique form to review your feedback. If there's something you don't understand, be sure to ask about it.

Message Preparation   (50%) _____

Presentation Plan & Bibliography, Note cards   (10%) _____

Message Delivery   (40%)_____

Speech Grade   _____

<u>Notes -- Overall strengths and suggestions for next speech:</u>

Concept Speech -- Critique Form Speaker _____

Missing, Ineffective, Satisfactory, Good, Excellent *Notes*

Competencies	*Part I: Message Preparation -- Appropriate for speaker, topic, audience, occasion, and purpose*	M	I	S	G	E
Topic	Chooses and narrows a topic					
	Meets general purpose – to inform					
Support/ Organization	Uses an organization pattern					
	* **Intro** – Uses attention-getter; identifies topic & purpose; establishes relevance & credibility; **previews main points**; transitions to 1ˢᵗ main point					
	* **Body** -- Provides appropriate supporting material with vivid and specific details – use of testimony, facts, examples					
	* use of transitions within the speech					
	***Presentation aid** – Design of effective presentation aid					
	Conclusion -- Restatement of thesis; memorable thought					
	Part I: Overall					
	Part II Energetic Message Delivery – Appropriate for audience, occasion, and purpose	M	I	S	G	E
Language	Uses appropriate language for the designated audience					
	*Effective Oral citation of sources					
Voice	***Variety** -- Uses vocal variety in volume, rate, pitch & intensity to heighten and maintain interest.					
	Accuracy -- Uses pronunciation, grammar, & articulation; minimizes filler words.					
Physical Behaviors	***Manner, movement and gestures** – Assertive stance; Uses movement and gestures effectively					
	Facial expression and eye contact -- Uses facial expressiveness and eye contact to support the message and engage with listeners					
	Presentation aid -- Effectively presents presentation aid to enhance message					
	Note cards – Effectively uses appropriately designed note cards to support speech					
Time?	*Part II: Overall*					

*****Focal points for this presentation** – all addressed in the reading for this unit

Notes:

Concept Speech -- Critique Form   Speaker _____

Competencies	Part I: Message Preparation -- Appropriate for speaker, topic, audience, occasion, and purpose	M	I	S	G	E
Topic	Chooses and narrows a topic					
	Meets general purpose – to inform					
Support/ Organization	Uses an organization pattern					
	* **Intro** – Uses attention-getter; identifies topic & purpose; establishes relevance & credibility; **previews main points**; transitions to 1ˢ main point					
	* **Body** -- Provides appropriate supporting material with vivid and specific details – use of testimony, facts, examples					
	* use of transitions within the speech					
	* **Presentation aid** – Design of effective presentation aid					
	Conclusion -- Restatement of thesis; memorable thought					
	Part I: Overall					
	Part II Energetic Message Delivery – Appropriate for audience, occasion, and purpose	M	I	S	G	E
Language	Uses appropriate language for the designated audience					
	*Effective Oral citation of sources					
Voice	* **Variety** -- Uses vocal variety in volume, rate, pitch & intensity to heighten and maintain interest.					
	Accuracy -- Uses pronunciation, grammar, & articulation; minimizes filler words.					
Physical Behaviors	* **Manner, movement and gestures** – Assertive stance; Uses movement and gestures effectively					
	Facial expression and eye contact -- Uses facial expressiveness and eye contact to support the message and engage with listeners					
	Presentation aid -- Effectively presents presentation aid to enhance message					
	Note cards – Effectively uses appropriately designed note cards to support speech					
Time?	*Part II: Overall*					

Missing, Ineffective, Satisfactory, Good, Excellent *Notes*

*Focal points for this presentation – all addressed in the reading for this unit

Notes – Strengths?

-- Areas for improvement   Critiqued by _____

Concept Speech -- Critique Form

Speaker _____

Competencies	Part I: Message Preparation -- Appropriate for speaker, topic, audience, occasion, and purpose	M	I	S	G	E
Topic	Chooses and narrows a topic					
	Meets general purpose – to inform					
Support/ Organization	Uses an organization pattern					
	* **Intro** – Uses attention-getter; identifies topic & purpose; establishes relevance & credibility; **previews main points**; transitions to 1ˢᵗ main point					
	* **Body** -- Provides appropriate supporting material with vivid and specific details – use of testimony, facts, examples					
	* use of transitions within the speech					
	***Presentation aid** – Design of effective presentation aid					
	Conclusion -- Restatement of thesis; memorable thought					
	Part I: Overall					
	Part II Energetic Message Delivery – Appropriate for audience, occasion, and purpose	M	I	S	G	E
Language	Uses appropriate language for the designated audience					
	*Effective Oral citation of sources					
Voice	***Variety** -- Uses vocal variety in volume, rate, pitch & intensity to heighten and maintain interest.					
	Accuracy -- Uses pronunciation, grammar, & articulation; minimizes filler words.					
Physical Behaviors	***Manner, movement and gestures** – Assertive stance; Uses movement and gestures effectively					
	Facial expression and eye contact -- Uses facial expressiveness and eye contact to support the message and engage with listeners					
	Presentation aid -- Effectively presents presentation aid to enhance message					
	Note cards – Effectively uses appropriately designed note cards to support speech					
Time?	*Part II: Overall*					

Missing, Ineffective, Satisfactory, Good, Excellent *Notes*

*Focal points for this presentation – all addressed in the reading for this unit

Notes – Strengths?

-- Areas for improvement?

Critiqued by _____

Concept Speech -- Critique Form

Speaker _____

Competencies	Part I: Message Preparation -- Appropriate for speaker, topic, audience, occasion, and purpose	M	I	S	G	E
		Missing, Ineffective, Satisfactory, Good, Excellent *Notes*				
Topic	Chooses and narrows a topic					
	Meets general purpose – to inform					
Support/ Organization	Uses an organization pattern					
	* **Intro** – Uses attention-getter; identifies topic & purpose; establishes relevance & credibility; **previews main points**; transitions to 1ˢᵗ main point					
	* **Body** -- Provides appropriate supporting material with vivid and specific details – use of testimony, facts, examples					
	* use of transitions within the speech					
	***Presentation aid** – Design of effective presentation aid					
	Conclusion -- Restatement of thesis; memorable thought					
	Part I: Overall					
	Part II *Energetic* Message Delivery – *Appropriate for audience, occasion, and purpose*	M	I	S	G	E
Language	Uses appropriate language for the designated audience					
	*Effective Oral citation of sources					
Voice	***Variety** -- Uses vocal variety in volume, rate, pitch & intensity to heighten and maintain interest.					
	Accuracy -- Uses pronunciation, grammar, & articulation; minimizes filler words.					
Physical Behaviors	***Manner, movement and gestures** – Assertive stance; Uses movement and gestures effectively					
	Facial expression and eye contact -- Uses facial expressiveness and eye contact to support the message and engage with listeners					
	Presentation aid -- Effectively presents presentation aid to enhance message					
	Note cards – Effectively uses appropriately designed note cards to support speech					
Time?	*Part II: Overall*					

*Focal points for this presentation** – all addressed in the reading for this unit

Notes – Strengths?

-- Areas for improvement?

Critiqued by _____

Concept Speech -- Critique Form   Speaker _____

Competencies	*Part I: Message Preparation -- Appropriate for speaker, topic, audience, occasion, and purpose*	M	I	S	G	E
Topic	Chooses and narrows a topic					
	Meets general purpose – to inform					
Support/ Organization	Uses an organization pattern					
	* **Intro** – Uses attention-getter; identifies topic & purpose; establishes relevance & credibility; **previews main points**; transitions to 1ˢᵗ main point					
	* **Body** -- Provides appropriate supporting material with vivid and specific details – use of testimony, facts, examples					
	* use of transitions within the speech					
	***Presentation aid** – Design of effective presentation aid					
	Conclusion -- Restatement of thesis; memorable thought					
	Part I: Overall					
	Part II Energetic Message Delivery – Appropriate for audience, occasion, and purpose	M	I	S	G	E
Language	Uses appropriate language for the designated audience					
	*Effective Oral citation of sources					
Voice	***Variety** -- Uses vocal variety in volume, rate, pitch & intensity to heighten and maintain interest.					
	Accuracy -- Uses pronunciation, grammar, & articulation; minimizes filler words.					
Physical Behaviors	***Manner, movement and gestures** – Assertive stance; Uses movement and gestures effectively					
	Facial expression and eye contact -- Uses facial expressiveness and eye contact to support the message and engage with listeners					
	Presentation aid -- Effectively presents presentation aid to enhance message					
	Note cards – Effectively uses appropriately designed note cards to support speech					
Time?	*Part II: Overall*					

*****Focal points for this presentation** – all addressed in the reading for this unit

Notes – Strengths?

-- Areas for improvement?   Critiqued by _____

Unit III -- Progress Report

1. Reading	*Course Guide* – Unit III Ch. 5 -- Ethics Ch. 6 -- Audience Analysis Ch.15 &16—Conclusions & Language Ch. 21 & 22 -- Presentation Aids Appendix E: Handling Questions & Answers Sample speeches--Canvas and p. 333 O'Hair
2. Quiz	*Course Guide; Chapters 5, 6, 15, 16, 21, 22* and App. E; *sample speeches*
3. Participation	REAL PS 3 Online and in-class activities
4. Speech	Progress Report

REAL PS 3 -- Progress Report
>   **R**esearch -- Combining personal expertise with authoritative source
>   **E**thics -- Selective use of detail to present accurate picture of project
>   **A**nalysis -- Analysis of audience and speech context
>   **L**anguage/Listening – Appropriate language for stakeholders chosen as audience
>   – Listening to prepare for Q&A

Academic and professional speakers are often required to give progress reports, and they have many decisions to make about the types of materials to include. Clearly, their ethical approach is important as they inform an audience about the status of a project.

Speech 3 -- Progress Report

Your next speaking assignment will enable you to practice developing and presenting a progress report to a group of interested listeners. You will be choosing a project with which you are involved, such as a research project or social event, or a campus project, such as a new building or policy.

Progress reports are used to describe the progress of a long-term project and are standard in all professions and organizations. The President gives a State of the Union Address, a programmer reports to his or her client, a civil engineer describes the progress on a project to the transportation officials, faculty report on their progress toward fulfilling the requirements of a grant, the city manager offers a progress report to the City Council about progress on the new court building, and marketing professionals report on the progress of the latest ad campaign.

Progress reports can be mandatory or voluntary in various organizations, and often a series of progress reports is prepared as a project moves through various stages. Such reports can be written at the beginning, mid-point, and/or the conclusion of a project. Sometimes we offer to develop progress reports just to be sure that our bosses know where we stand with a project. In some organizations, professionals write such reports and deliver them to those in authority, but very often a progress report is delivered as a speech to an audience of stakeholders.

Ethical considerations are crucial because you must give your audience a true picture of the progress on a project even if you might want to present only positive information.

Because of the widespread use of progress reports, certainly it's important for students in Public Speaking to get some practice with this type of presentation!

Guidelines for Speech 3

Complexity	Level 3 -- includes levels 1 and 2
Type	Progress; extemporaneous
Topic choice/focus	Status of project on which you are working or have worked -- class project, volunteer work, professional project, etc.
Audience	Group of stakeholders or interested parties who need information about the project
Purpose	Inform
Credibility	Personal expertise as participant; choice of valid and appropriate sources local and/or library sources
Support	• Examples, testimony, facts and/or statistics • Minimum of 2 sources (such as brochures, policy manuals, articles) • Source citation: written bibliography **and** oral citation *Note: Insufficient oral citation will result in point deduction.*
Organization	Chronological; topical Emphasis on effective conclusions
Voice & language	Language appropriate for audience
Physical behaviors	Management of technology; variety of physical strategies
Presentation aids	2-4 PowerPoint slides (plus spacer slides) PowerPoint should enhance your speech, not repeat it.
Time	4 ½ -6 minutes + Q&A
Note cards	Maximum -- 4 4x6 cards

Speech preparation and delivery

Successful presentations will necessitate the completion of the following steps:

- **Invention**
  - o Choose an appropriate topic
  - o Identify audience and determine audience needs
  - o Generate supporting detail, based on your own knowledge and other credible sources
- **Arrangement**
  - o Organize intro progress report style
  - o Develop speech plan
- **Style**
  - o Choose language appropriate for audience
  - o Choose detail appropriate for audience
- **Memory and Delivery**
  - o Prepare PowerPoint slides
  - o Rehearse -- focus on vocal variety and use of PowerPoint
  - o Present, using no more than 4 4x6 note cards

Related writing

- Presentation plan/outline
- Critiques of peers' speeches

Topic

The topic for this speech should involve (1) a project you are or have been involved in (in a class, in a social organization, or as a volunteer) or (2) one which affects the VT campus or the Blacksburg community, such as the construction of a building, the development of a new policy, or the work of a committee on a specific initiative. The progress report can address a project that is just starting, one that you're in the middle of, or one that has been completed.

Topic Possibilities -- Progress Report

As you consider your speech, brainstorm to create a list of at least 10 projects in which you are or have been involved.

Try responding to these prompts as you make notes. Don't judge the possibilities; just write whatever comes to mind.

- List 2 or 3 academic projects for a class -- reports? research?
- List 2 or 3 professional projects -- internships? career-related job? study abroad?
- List 2 or 3 volunteer/social projects -- organizing a blood drive? managing an activity for your social group/club/fraternity-sorority? service learning?
- List 2 or 3 university-related projects (related to your campus job or volunteer effort) -- layout for the CT, promotional videos for VT, service on a university committee
- List 2 or 3 personal projects -- church youth group?

Continue listing projects in which you have an administrative role -- the kind of project you would need to report on to a group of stakeholders. Choose the 2 or 3 topics that seem to be the best fit for this assignment. Don't make a final decision until you determine an audience and an occasion so that you can make this speech as realistic as possible.

Audience identification and analysis

Once you decide on a project to review for your speech, consider the audience. What group of folks is likely to be interested in the progress of this project? Who are the stakeholders to whom you might report? **Note:** When you give your speech, you'll ask your classmates to put themselves in the position of this target audience.

The audience must be more than one person! What group has invested in your project? What group is going to be affected by your project? What group will be interested in your success? Consider a panel of faculty who would be interested in your research, the membership of your organization, internship supervisors, campus administrators, neighbors of your apartment complex, etc.

As you read the chapter on audience analysis, begin to consider the characteristics of this group of people. What is their background? Why do they care about your project? Are they in favor of your project? How old are they? We'll discuss some of these characteristics in class.

This analysis is crucial because so many subsequent decisions will hinge on the characteristics of this group. After all, your progress report is for them, so your supporting materials, organization, language and visuals should be selected with these listeners in mind.

Then consider the type of occasion at which a situation might be given -- such as, a meeting of your organization? Graduation symposium? Service learning seminar? City council meeting?

Progress Report Speech – Audience Analysis – Type and submit as instructed.
Report on the following decisions once you have determined the focus of this progress
report.

I. At what type of meeting would I give this speech?
Academic committee? monthly meeting of a campus organization? update to employers?
report on research project to a class? PTA or City Council meeting?

II. Who would attend this meeting? Audience Analysis (Chapter 6)
- Disposition (O'Hair, p. 85)? What do they already know about your project? What is
their attitude toward the project?
- Demographics (O'Hair, p. 87)?

III. How will I appeal to my audience? (O'Hair, p. 85)

IV. Research
- What types of research will I include?
Interviews? Brochures? CT articles? (See section below.)
- How will that research build my credibility? (Ethics, Ch. 5, O'Hair)

Research Possibilities
The research for this speech need not involve library research. Consider your experience
and include references to people or materials you encountered during the project. You might
consider any of the following types of evidence for this speech.
Appendix B and Appendix C in O'Hair include samples of bibliography form; choose
examples that most closely resemble the sources you're using. Each example below is followed
by a suggestion for bibliography format based on APA documentation or Chicago
documentation." Either format is acceptable; just be consistent.

1. **Expert Testimony** -- You might interview an expert who had some oversight of the
project, such as your internship director, the manager of the construction project, your church
youth coordinator, or a policy-maker on campus. This expert would not be a member of your
intended audience, rather someone who has direct knowledge of the project.
APA -- For interview or email, use interviewee's name first, such as the following with
"Smith" as the name of the interviewee:
Smith, J. (20 March 2017). Personal interview with construction manager.
Blacksburg, VA.

2. **Peer Testimony --** You might want to include comments from a peer who was also
involved with the project. Be careful to use this kind of testimony sparingly. Usually peers don't
have a sense of the entire project and can comment only on the experience from a personal
perspective.
Same format as above.

3. **Promotional Materials** -- Brochures, programs, organizational website with background info (Note: Use only organizational websites, not personal websites as resources for this speech.)

Brochures -- use same format as book with as much information as possible. The author might be the organization rather than an individual. For example (in APA format),

American Red Cross. (2017 May). Donating your time to save lives. [Brochure]
Red Cross Headquarters. Blacksburg, VA.
APA, F #10 – document from a website

4. **Policy/Legal Information** -- Bylaws of an organization, laws that might regulate the size or placement of an event, policies of the university
APA, F #4 -- government document

5. **Local newspapers** -- The *Collegiate Times* or *The Roanoke Times* might be good sources for any local projects.
APA, F #8 -- newspaper article

Certainly any of the standard types of sources -- books or journals -- could work for this project. Refer to the Appendix B or C for models of documentation.

Managing Questions and Answers

O'Hair offers strategies for Q&A in Appendix E. Be sure to take advantage of those strategies. In addition, plan ahead to save the last line of your speech for the end of Q&A. Don't let your speech end with a question or response -- something that might even sidetrack your audience from the focal point of your speech.

Protocol for Q & A
1. Summarize main ideas and reiterate thesis and then ask for questions.
2. Repeat or rephrase the question to make sure you understood it and so the rest of the audience gets a chance to hear it. You might include the topic of the question in the answer.
3. Start answer by making eye contact with questioner, and then move to rest of audience.
4. Don't be afraid to pause a moment while you formulate your answer.
5. Be concise in your answer; don't give another speech.
6. Don't "wing it." If you don't know the answer, say, "I'm not sure, but I will get back to you on that."
7. After questions, close speech with impact.

Presentation Plan -- Keyword Outline
> Your presentation plan and bibliography will be evaluated by your instructor as part of "message preparation." Use the "speaking outline" format, O'Hair p. 212A

Message:
Audience:
Purpose: To inform _____

Introduction
> A. Gain attention
> B. Introduce purpose and topic
> C. Motivate audience -- establish relevance of info and speaker credibility
> D. Preview main points

Transition to 1ˢᵗ main point

I. Background of project -- Describe the purpose of the project and offer whatever explanation is appropriate for the audience you've chosen.
> A.
> > 1.
> > 2.
> B.

(transition)

II. Work Completed -- What stages of the project have been completed? How well did that work match the original plan? Were there unexpected problems or delays or expenses?
> A.
> B.

(transition)

III. Present Status -- What is the current phase that is in production? Have any adjustments been made that affect the current work?
> A.
> B.

(transition)

IV. Work Remaining -- What steps of the project are yet to be completed? What are your expectations? What do you want to accomplish? Have you revised your plan? Why? Is the original deadline still feasible? Explain why or why not.
> A.
> B.

(transition)

Conclusion – Comment on effectiveness of the project, summary of accomplishment or cautions (O'Hair, Chapter 15; see checklist, p. 227) Don't introduce new ideas! Ask for questions. Provide final thought when Q&A ends.

Note: Short bibliography may be listed at end of outline rather than on separate page.

Name _____

Instructor Summary of Feedback -- Progress Report

Please attach this form to your presentation plan; the critique for instructor's use is on the back of this page. The outline must be available to your instructor before you can give your speech.

After your speech, your instructor will review his or her notes on a critique form and any forms that your peers completed about your speech. Your instructor might use ✓ , ✓ + or ✓ - on some of the lines below to show your general accomplishment in the areas listed. When the papers are returned to you, please use this form along with the instructor critique form to review your feedback. If there's something you don't understand, be sure to ask about it.

Message Preparation   (50%) _____
    Based on careful decisions about audience and context

    Outline, Bibliography, Audience Analysis; Notecards   (10%) _____

Message Delivery   (40%) _____

Speech Grade   _____

Notes -- Overall strengths and suggestions for next speech:

Progress Report -- Critique Form   Speaker _____

Missing, Ineffective, Satisfactory, Good, Excellent *Notes*

Competencies	*Part I: Message Preparation -- Appropriate for speaker, topic, audience, occasion, and purpose*	M	I	S	G	E
Topic	Chooses and narrows a topic					
	*Careful connection with audience needs/interests					
	Meets general purpose					
Support/ Organization	Uses an organization pattern					
	Intro – Uses attention-getter; identifies topic & purpose; establishes relevance & credibility; previews main points; transitions to 1ᵗ main point					
	Body -- *Provides appropriate supporting material with vivid and specific details (Background; Work completed; Present status; Work remaining)					
	Use of transitions within the speech					
	***Presentation aid** -- Design of effective PowerPoint					
	***Conclusion --** Restatement of thesis; memorable thought					
	Part I: Overall					
	Part II Energetic Message Delivery – Appropriate for audience, occasion, and purpose	M	I	S	G	E
Language	*Uses appropriate language for the designated audience					
	*Effective oral citation of sources					
Voice	**Variety --** Uses vocal variety in volume, rate, pitch & intensity to heighten and maintain interest.					
	Accuracy -- Uses pronunciation, grammar, & articulation; minimizes filler words.					
Physical Behaviors	**Manner, movement and gestures –** Uses assertive stance; Uses movement and gestures effectively					
	Facial expression and eye contact -- Uses facial expressiveness and eye contact to support the message and engage with listeners					
	***Presentation aid--**Effectively presents Power-Point to enhance speech (not repeat message)					
	Note cards – Effectively uses appropriately designed note cards to support speech					
Q&A	* **Effective management of Q&A** (Restated/rephrased question)					
Time?	*Part II: Overall*					

***Focal points for this speech – addressed in the reading and homework for this unit*

Notes --

Progress Report -- Critique Form   Speaker _____

Missing, Ineffective, Satisfactory, Good, Excellent *Notes*

Competencies	Part I: Message Preparation -- Appropriate for speaker, topic, audience, occasion, and purpose	M	I	S	G	E
Topic	Chooses and narrows a topic					
	*Careful connection with audience needs/interests					
	Meets general purpose					
Support/ Organization	Uses an organization pattern					
	Intro – Uses attention-getter; identifies topic & purpose; establishes relevance & credibility; previews main points; transitions to 1ˢᵗ main point					
	Body -- *Provides appropriate supporting material with vivid and specific details (Background; Work completed; Present status; Work remaining)					
	Use of transitions within the speech					
	***Presentation aid** -- Design of effective PowerPoint					
	***Conclusion** -- Restatement of thesis; memorable thought					
	Part I: Overall					
	Part II Energetic Message Delivery – Appropriate for audience, occasion, and purpose	M	I	S	G	E
Language	*Uses appropriate language for the designated audience					
	*Effective oral citation of sources					
Voice	**Variety** -- Uses vocal variety in volume, rate, pitch & intensity to heighten and maintain interest.					
	Accuracy -- Uses pronunciation, grammar, & articulation; minimizes filler words.					
Physical Behaviors	**Manner, movement and gestures** – Uses assertive stance; Uses movement and gestures effectively					
	Facial expression and eye contact -- Uses facial expressiveness and eye contact to support the message and engage with listeners					
	***Presentation aid**--Effectively presents Power-Point to enhance speech (not repeat message)					
	Note cards – Effectively uses appropriately designed note cards to support speech					
Q&A	* **Effective management of Q&A** (Restated/rephrased question)					
Time?	*Part II: Overall*					

*Focal points for this speech – addressed in the reading and homework for this unit

Strengths?

Areas for improvement?   Critiqued by _____

Progress Report -- Critique Form   Speaker _____

Competencies	Part I: Message Preparation -- Appropriate for speaker, topic, audience, occasion, and purpose	M	I	S	G	E
Topic	Chooses and narrows a topic					
	*Careful connection with audience needs/interests					
	Meets general purpose					
Support/ Organization	Uses an organization pattern					
	Intro – Uses attention-getter; identifies topic & purpose; establishes relevance & credibility; previews main points; transitions to 1st main point					
	Body -- *Provides appropriate supporting material with vivid and specific details (Background; Work completed; Present status; Work remaining)					
	Use of transitions within the speech					
	*Presentation aid -- Design of effective PowerPoint					
	*Conclusion -- Restatement of thesis; memorable thought					
	Part I: Overall					
	Part II Energetic Message Delivery – Appropriate for audience, occasion, and purpose	M	I	S	G	E
Language	*Uses appropriate language for the designated audience					
	*Effective oral citation of sources					
Voice	Variety -- Uses vocal variety in volume, rate, pitch & intensity to heighten and maintain interest.					
	Accuracy -- Uses pronunciation, grammar, & articulation; minimizes filler words.					
Physical Behaviors	Manner, movement and gestures – Uses assertive stance; Uses movement and gestures effectively					
	Facial expression and eye contact -- Uses facial expressiveness and eye contact to support the message and engage with listeners					
	*Presentation aid--Effectively presents Power-Point to enhance speech (not repeat message)					
	Note cards – Effectively uses appropriately designed note cards to support speech					
Q&A	* Effective management of Q&A (Restated/rephrased question)					
Time?	Part II: Overall					

Missing, Ineffective, Satisfactory, Good, Excellent *Notes*

Focal points for this speech – addressed in the reading and homework for this unit

Strengths?

Areas for improvement?   Critiqued by _____

Progress Report -- Critique Form

Speaker _____

Competencies	Part I: Message Preparation -- Appropriate for speaker, topic, audience, occasion, and purpose	M	I	S	G	E
Topic	Chooses and narrows a topic					
	*Careful connection with audience needs/interests					
	Meets general purpose					
Support/ Organization	Uses an organization pattern					
	Intro – Uses attention-getter; identifies topic & purpose; establishes relevance & credibility; previews main points; transitions to 1ˢᵗ main point					
	Body -- *Provides appropriate supporting material with vivid and specific details (Background; Work completed; Present status; Work remaining)					
	Use of transitions within the speech					
	***Presentation aid** -- Design of effective PowerPoint					
	***Conclusion** -- Restatement of thesis; memorable thought					
	Part I: Overall					
	Part II Energetic Message Delivery – Appropriate for audience, occasion, and purpose	M	I	S	G	E
Language	*Uses appropriate language for the designated audience					
	*Effective oral citation of sources					
Voice	**Variety** -- Uses vocal variety in volume, rate, pitch & intensity to heighten and maintain interest.					
	Accuracy -- Uses pronunciation, grammar, & articulation; minimizes filler words.					
Physical Behaviors	**Manner, movement and gestures** – Uses assertive stance; Uses movement and gestures effectively					
	Facial expression and eye contact -- Uses facial expressiveness and eye contact to support the message and engage with listeners					
	***Presentation aid**--Effectively presents Power-Point to enhance speech (not repeat message)					
	Note cards – Effectively uses appropriately designed note cards to support speech					
Q&A	* **Effective management of Q&A** (Restated/rephrased question)					
Time?	*Part II: Overall*					

Missing, Ineffective, Satisfactory, Good, Excellent **Notes**

Focal points for this speech – addressed in the reading and homework for this unit

Strengths?

Areas for improvement?

Critiqued by _____

Progress Report -- Critique Form   Speaker _____

Competencies	Part I: Message Preparation -- Appropriate for speaker, topic, audience, occasion, and purpose	M	I	S	G	E
Topic	Chooses and narrows a topic					
	*Careful connection with audience needs/interests					
	Meets general purpose					
Support/ Organization	Uses an organization pattern					
	Intro – Uses attention-getter; identifies topic & purpose; establishes relevance & credibility; previews main points; transitions to 1ˢᵗ main point					
	Body -- *Provides appropriate supporting material with vivid and specific details (Background; Work completed; Present status; Work remaining)					
	Use of transitions within the speech					
	*Presentation aid -- Design of effective PowerPoint					
	*Conclusion -- Restatement of thesis; memorable thought					
	Part I: Overall					
	Part II Energetic Message Delivery – Appropriate for audience, occasion, and purpose	M	I	S	G	E
Language	*Uses appropriate language for the designated audience					
	*Effective oral citation of sources					
Voice	Variety -- Uses vocal variety in volume, rate, pitch & intensity to heighten and maintain interest.					
	Accuracy -- Uses pronunciation, grammar, & articulation; minimizes filler words.					
Physical Behaviors	Manner, movement and gestures – Uses assertive stance; Uses movement and gestures effectively					
	Facial expression and eye contact -- Uses facial expressiveness and eye contact to support the message and engage with listeners					
	*Presentation aid--Effectively presents Power-Point to enhance speech (not repeat message)					
	Note cards – Effectively uses appropriately designed note cards to support speech					
Q&A	* Effective management of Q&A (Restated/rephrased question)					
Time?	Part II: Overall					

Missing, Ineffective, Satisfactory, Good, Excellent *Notes*

Focal points for this speech – addressed in the reading and homework for this unit

Strengths?

Areas for improvement?   Critiqued by _____

Unit IV -- Issue Analysis: Perspectives

1. Reading	*Course Guide* – Unit IV Ch. 9 -- Online research Ch. 12 -- Types of Organization Ch. 17 -- Methods of Delivery Ch. 20 – Using Presentation Aids Ch. 23 -- Informative Speech Ch. 25 -- Argument Sample speeches--Canvas and p. 483 O'Hair
2. Quiz	*Course Guide (*point & block organizational patterns*); Chapters* 9, 12, 17, 20 23, 25; p. 463; *sample speeches*
3. Participation	REAL PS 4 Online and in-class activities
4. Speech	Issue Analysis

REAL PS 4 --Issue Analysis: Perspectives
> **R**esearch -- Researching various perspectives
> **E**thics -- Building an argument
> **A**nalysis -- Analysis of Context (Setting, Audience, Occasion)
> **L**anguage/Listening -- Language to promote understanding (not emotional reaction); Listening for logical argument

Speakers who inform an audience about two or more sides of an issue have a tough role to play. They aren't trying to persuade the audience, so they have to be highly ethical in their approach -- not allowing personal biases to show.

Speech 4 – Issue Analysis: Perspectives on a Controversial Issue

This speech will allow you to analyze a controversy of your choice and present it to an audience who might need information about the controversy.

In your personal, academic, and professional life, controversies, problems, and disagreements will be obstacles to your goals. More than likely, you will have a strong point of view about the problems and controversies that influence your life and about the best way to improve those situations. Naturally, you will want people to see the situation "your way."

However, before you can effectively solve a problem or persuade people of your position, you will need to research the controversy and understand it from all angles and perspectives. Often professionals are asked to research both sides of an issue in order to help their employers or clients solve a problem.

By researching the topic using a variety of sources--including Virginia Tech's library databases--you will get a "big picture" view of the controversy. Avoid presenting just the evidence that fits your position on the controversy. Instead, present both sides of the issue in the same way a journalist or reporter might <u>objectively</u> describe the positions of clashing protesters. While the reporter might agree with one group, the resulting newspaper article can't reveal that preference. Similarly, the dean of your college might ask you to characterize student positions on a campus development. Again, the ultimate presentation can't show a preference for one position or the other; it should be informative, not persuasive.

Guidelines for Speech 4

Complexity	Level 4 -- includes levels 1, 2, and 3
Type	Issue analysis/perspectives -- extemporaneous style
Topic choice/focus	Controversial topic based on student interest, involvement, major
Audience	Audience who needs information about the controversy
Purpose	Inform -- Avoid a one-sided, biased view of the controversy
Credibility	• Personal interest/experience • Choice of credible, balanced sources
Support	• Examples, testimony, facts, statistics • Minimum of 4 sources from a variety of types of sources, including library databases • Source citation: written bibliography **and** oral citation *Note: Insufficient oral citation will result in point deduction.*
Organization	Comp-contrast, cause-effect, problem-solution, or topical
Voice & language	Appropriate vocal variety and language choices
Physical behaviors	Mastery of technology; variety of physical strategies
Presentation aids	4+ PowerPoint slides plus spacer slides (advanced)
Time	6 ½ -7 ½ minutes
Note cards	Maximum 5 4x6 cards

Speech preparation and delivery

Successful presentations will necessitate the completion of the following steps:

- **Invention**
    - o Choose an appropriate topic. Think about controversies on campus (e.g., football ticket lottery); controversies in your major; controversies in your apartment complex or home community. Choose a topic you already know about and are interested in researching further.
    - o Identify a speaking context and develop preliminary MAP.
    - o Determine audience needs.
    - o Generate supporting material from a variety of sources, including your prior knowledge and research from library databases. Research could also include primary sources (such as personal interviews).
- **Arrangement**
    - o Organize using a topical, cause-effect, or problem-solution organizational pattern. (See details about organization below.)
    - o Create a presentation plan.
- **Style**
    - o Choose language appropriate for audience
    - o Choose detail appropriate for audience
- **Memory and Delivery**
    - o Design and create minimum of four PowerPoint slides with at least one example of animation.
    - o Rehearse.
    - o Present, using 3 to 5 4X6 note cards (keywords only!)

Related writing

- Presentation plan and bibliography
- Critiques of peers' speeches

Topic Possibilities -- Issue Analysis: Providing Perspectives

As you consider possibilities for a controversial topic, be careful to select an issue you already know about and care about--something fresh and intriguing for you and for your audience. (Avoid over-used and too-complex topics, such as gun control, stem cell research, abortion, or legalization of marijuana.) Your expertise and enthusiasm are crucial!

Brainstorm a list of at least 10 possibilities. Use the following prompts to get started:

1. List 2-3 campus issues that are of concern to you -- new policies, potential buildings, tuition changes, etc.

2. List 2-3 controversies that affect the town of Blacksburg or your particular housing complex.

3. List 2-3 controversies in your major -- theoretical clashes, solutions for a particular problem, etc.

4. List 2-3 controversies in your home town -- plans to build a new shopping center? Zoning changes? Traffic changes?

5. List 2-3 local (city or state) political issues

Add more possibilities to your list before you make a choice to match the criteria for this assignment. In many cases, you have probably identified a problem for which there are various solutions. Be sure that you could identify and describe two different perspectives on the issue. The controversy should be current! See "context analysis" on the following page.

Audience of Stakeholders

Once you have chosen a topic, identify the various interested groups for whom you might develop a presentation. Once you choose a particular group, your analysis of those listeners will help you to decide on your research, your main points, your examples, your language, and even your organization.

For example, if you choose a controversy about VT tuition, you might identify numerous groups who could be interested -- administrators, incoming students, families of students, alumni, or even legislators. The effectiveness of your speech depends on your selection of a target group and your analysis of their needs, knowledge and concerns.

Research Possibilities

Use the library databases to round out your information about the subject -- NOT Wikipedia. Try searches of public information -- government publications, magazines, and newspapers. Of course, if you choose an audience of faculty or researchers, go back to the scholarly journals in your field.

Consider what types of publications will carry the most weight with your audience. What will your listeners view as credible?

Review the research information on the Canvas site.

Issue Analysis Speech – Context Analysis – Type and submit as instructed.

Reference: O'Hair, Chapters 6 and 7

Complete this analysis before working on your presentation plan. Review your responses with your instructor. The information below is a model only; see sample speaking outline p.212a.

Message:

Audience:

Purpose: To inform _____

1. Speech Occasion -- At what type of meeting would I give this speech?

(for example, town hall meeting in my community, stockholder meeting, academic conference, PTA, monthly meeting of a volunteer organization, meeting of a social organization)

2. Speaker-Listener Relationship
   - My expertise on this issue _____
   - Listeners' expertise -- Choose 1:
     o Listeners are experts in the general area, but I have greater expertise on this specific issue (example: presentation of senior thesis to faculty)
     o Listeners are peers who have same general background as I do, but I have greater expertise on this issue (example: co-workers on new-product team)
     o Listeners are involved/interested, but generally uninformed about this issue (community members attending meeting about new highway options)

3. Audience Analysis
   - Disposition
     o Toward topic
     o Toward speaker
     o Toward occasion
   - Demographics
     o Age, Gender
     o Ethnic or cultural background
     o Socioeconomic status
     o Religion, Political affiliations

4. Setting -- Checklist, O'Hair, p. 101

Adapting to Context – See Checklists
   - Narrowing the topic (p. 111)
   - Thesis statement (p. 117)
   - Audience Demographics (p. 92)

Considering Organization

Because this assignment requires a focus on different perspectives, its organization is more complex than the organization of previous speeches. In your text, you'll read about appropriate formats for organizing a speech, including cause-effect, problem-solution, and topical.

Once you have identified your audience and collected your research, you'll determine which pattern of organization will be appropriate for your MAP.

Since no one pattern will fit every speech, you'll find listed below some general plans you might choose from and adapt for your speaking needs.

Regardless of which of the three recommended patterns you choose, you need to consider the overarching nature of comparison-contrast. That is, you are presenting two sides of an issue, so you want your listeners to be able to recognize their commonalities and differences. Listeners will be confused by an "apples to oranges" approach that reveals different aspects of different perspectives. Rather, they need an "apples to apples" approach that compares the same aspects of different perspectives. Usually, speakers use the "point method" or the "block method" to accomplish this.

Topical Organization. The example below shows the organization a person might use if he or she were informing an audience about the goals of two political candidates, comparing candidate X to candidate Y. Although one outline looks longer than the other, each reflects the categories of information, presented in a consistent order -- one that is easy for a listener to grasp.

Topical organization by "point method"	**Topical organization by "block method"**
Intro	*Intro*
I. Political Goals	I. Candidate X
A. Candidate X	A. Political Goals
B. Candidate Y	B. Economic Goals
II. Economic Goals	C. Social Goals
A. Candidate X	II. Candidate Y
B. Candidate Y	A. Political Goals
III. Social Goals	B. Economic Goals
A. Candidate X	C. Social Goals
B. Candidate Y	*Conclusion*
Conclusion	

Problem-solution Organization. The example below shows the organization a person might use to compare two perspectives on the solution to a problem. Again the "point" or "block" method comes into play. This example shows examples of points that might be used for a particular speech. A speaker would certainly develop points appropriate to a topic, audience, and occasion. (Note: The discussion of the problem is brief because listeners would already know the problem; speaker can remind listeners of situation and further establish common ground.)

Problem-Solution by "point method"	**Problem-solution by "block method"**
Intro	*Intro*
I. Problem (brief)	I. Problem (brief)
A.	A.
B.	B.
II. Solution's Impact on Community	II. Solution X
A. Solution X	A. Impact on Community
B. Solution Y	B. Cost
III. Solution's Cost	C. Timeframe
A. Solution X	III. Solution Y
B. Solution Y	A. Impact on Community
IV. Solution's Timeframe	B. Cost
A, Solution X	C. Timeframe
B. Solution Y	*Conclusion*
Conclusion	

Cause-effect Organization. If your speech will address causes or effects, again the point-block consideration works. This example reflects outlines used to discuss the effects of a particular cause. The listeners already understand the cause, so it is explained briefly as a reminder and a way of establishing agreement. For example, researchers disagree about the effect of early "academic" stimulation with babies. The audience might be parents of newborns who are deciding whether or not to invest in such flash cards for two-year olds.

Cause-effect by "point method"
Intro
I. Cause
    A.
    B.
II. Cognitive functioning
    A. Effect X
    B. Effect Y
III. Future school performance
    A. Effect X
    B. Effect Y
IV. Future professional performance
    A. Effect X
    B. Effect Y
Conclusion

Cause-effect by "block method"
Intro
I. Cause -- Early Academic Stimulation
    A.
    B.
II. Effect X -- Enhanced intelligence
    A. Cognitive functioning
    B. Future school performance
    C. Future professional performance
III. Effect Y -- Reduced creativity
    A. Cognitive functioning
    B. Future school performance
    C. Future professional performance
Conclusion

While the outline above focuses on effects, you could also create a speech that focuses on causes. For example, an audience is aware of and concerned about climate change, but they don't know that experts differ on the causes of that climate change. Of course, you wouldn't choose such a broad topic, but a speaker could briefly discuss the effect (climate change) and discuss two different perspectives about the causes: Cause X and Cause Y. Either the block method or the point method could work.

Building an Argument

As you make a case for each side of the issue, you should build a solid argument, based on a **claim** you make, the **data/evidence** you provide to support the claim, and the **warrant** -- your connection of the claim and data. See the explanation of these components in O'Hair, Ch. 25.

When you explain each side of the issue, you'll explain the main points. What do the people on each side believe is true? (Claim) What evidence is used to prove the truth of that point? (Evidence/Data) How do they explain the link between the claim and the evidence?

Be careful! Don't slip into persuasion by arguing in some emotional, aggressive fashion. Rather, you should present logical arguments for each side of the issue, so that each is credible to your audience.

Issue Analysis: Presentation Plan

Your presentation plan, bibliography, and context analysis will be evaluated as part of your "message preparation." Please refer to the three organization examples on the previous pages and follow accordingly.

MAP:

My goal for this speech based on feedback from previous speeches:

Introduction
- Attention-getter
- Introduce topic and purpose
- Motivate – credibility and relevance
- Preview

Transition to 1ˢ main point

Body
- Choose appropriate organizational pattern (point or block?) – see organizational possibilities on the previous page
- Include well developed arguments to substantiate various perspectives (O'Hair, p. 358) – What is the claim made by people who hold each perspective? What evidence do they use to support that claim?
- Use fully developed keyword outline form
- Show transitions and indicate use of sources

Conclusion
- Use a transition to the conclusion; signal the close of the speech (without saying "In conclusion")
- Summarize main points and/or reiterate topic and purpose
- Challenge audience to respond

Bibliography with standard documentation format such as the following:
- APA, Appendix C

Unit IV Notes

Name _____

Instructor Summary of Feedback -- Issue Analysis

Please attach this form to your outline; the critique for instructor's use is on the back of this page. The outline must be available to your instructor before you can give your speech.

After your speech, your instructor will review his or her notes on a critique form and any forms that your peers completed about your speech. Your instructor might use ✓ , ✓ + or ✓ - on some of the lines below to show your general accomplishment in the areas listed. When the papers are returned to you, please use this form along with the instructor critique form to review your feedback. If there's something you don't understand, be sure to ask about it.

Message Preparation   (50%)_____

Context analysis, outline & bibliography   (10%)_____
      Note cards

Message Delivery   (40%)_____

Speech Grade   _____

Notes – Overall strengths, growth, and consideration for future speaking situations:

Issue Analysis -- Critique Form

Speaker _____

Competencies	Part I: Message Preparation -- Appropriate for speaker, topic, audience, occasion, and purpose	M	I	S	G	E
Topic	Chooses and narrows a topic					
	Meets general purpose – to inform					
Support/ Organization	**Intro –** Uses attention-getter; identifies topic & purpose; establishes relevance & credibility; previews main points; transitions to 1ˢᵗ main point					
	Body -- *Chooses appropriate supporting material to support **each** perspective					
	*Ethically and objectively constructs an argument for each perspective					
	*Uses appropriate comparison/contrast organization & transitions (point or block method)					
	***Presentation aid** – appropriate design of advanced PowerPoint					
	Conclusion -- Restatement of thesis; memorable thought					
	Part I: Overall					
	Part II Energetic Message Delivery – Appropriate for audience, occasion, and purpose	M	I	S	G	E
Language	Uses appropriate language for the designated audience					
	Effective oral citation of sources					
Voice	**Variety --** Uses vocal variety in volume, rate, pitch & intensity to heighten and maintain interest.					
	Accuracy -- Uses pronunciation, grammar, & articulation; minimizes filler words.					
Physical Behaviors	**Manner, movement and gestures** – Uses assertive stance; Uses movement and gestures effectively					
	Facial expression and eye contact -- Uses facial expressiveness and eye contact to support the message and engage with listeners					
	***Presentation aid --** Effectively presents advanced PowerPoint to enhance speech (not repeat message)					
	Note cards – Effectively uses appropriately designed note cards to support speech					
Time?	*Part II: Overall*					

The header above the M I S G E columns reads: Missing, Ineffective, Satisfactory, Good, Excellent *Notes*

*** Focal points for this speech** – addressed in reading and homework*

Notes

Issue Analysis -- Critique Form

Speaker _____

Competencies	Part I: Message Preparation -- Appropriate for speaker, topic, audience, occasion, and purpose	M	I	S	G	E
Topic	Chooses and narrows a topic					
	Meets general purpose – to inform					
Support/ Organization	Intro – Uses attention-getter; identifies topic & purpose; establishes relevance & credibility; previews main points; transitions to 1ˢᵗ main point					
	Body -- *Chooses appropriate supporting material to support each perspective					
	*Ethically and objectively constructs an argument for each perspective					
	*Uses appropriate comparison/contrast organization & transitions (point or block method)					
	*Presentation aid – appropriate design of advanced PowerPoint					
	Conclusion -- Restatement of thesis; memorable thought					
	Part I: Overall					
	Part II Energetic Message Delivery – Appropriate for audience, occasion, and purpose	M	I	S	G	E
Language	Uses appropriate language for the designated audience					
	Effective oral citation of sources					
Voice	Variety -- Uses vocal variety in volume, rate, pitch & intensity to heighten and maintain interest.					
	Accuracy -- Uses pronunciation, grammar, & articulation; minimizes filler words.					
Physical Behaviors	Manner, movement and gestures – Uses assertive stance; Uses movement and gestures effectively					
	Facial expression and eye contact -- Uses facial expressiveness and eye contact to support the message and engage with listeners					
	*Presentation aid -- Effectively presents advanced PowerPoint to enhance speech (not repeat message)					
	Note cards – Effectively uses appropriately designed note cards to support speech					
Time?	Part II: Overall					

The header above the M I S G E columns reads: Missing, Ineffective, Satisfactory, Good, Excellent **Notes**

* **Focal points for this speech –** *addressed in reading and homework*
Notes – Strengths?   Areas for improvement?

Critiqued by _____

Issue Analysis -- Critique Form

Speaker _____

Competencies	Part I: Message Preparation -- Appropriate for speaker, topic, audience, occasion, and purpose	M	I	S	G	E
Topic	Chooses and narrows a topic					
	Meets general purpose – to inform					
Support/ Organization	Intro – Uses attention-getter; identifies topic & purpose; establishes relevance & credibility; previews main points; transitions to 1ˢᵗ main point					
	Body -- *Chooses appropriate supporting material to support each perspective					
	*Ethically and objectively constructs an argument for each perspective					
	*Uses appropriate comparison/contrast organization & transitions (point or block method)					
	*Presentation aid – appropriate design of advanced PowerPoint					
	Conclusion -- Restatement of thesis; memorable thought					
	Part I: Overall					
	Part II Energetic Message Delivery – Appropriate for audience, occasion, and purpose	M	I	S	G	E
Language	Uses appropriate language for the designated audience					
	Effective oral citation of sources					
Voice	Variety -- Uses vocal variety in volume, rate, pitch & intensity to heighten and maintain interest.					
	Accuracy -- Uses pronunciation, grammar, & articulation; minimizes filler words.					
Physical Behaviors	Manner, movement and gestures – Uses assertive stance; Uses movement and gestures effectively					
	Facial expression and eye contact -- Uses facial expressiveness and eye contact to support the message and engage with listeners					
	*Presentation aid -- Effectively presents advanced PowerPoint to enhance speech (not repeat message)					
	Note cards – Effectively uses appropriately designed note cards to support speech					
Time?	Part II: Overall					

Missing, Ineffective, Satisfactory, Good, Excellent *Notes*

* Focal points for this speech – addressed in reading and homework
Notes – Strengths? Areas for improvement?

Critiqued by _____

Issue Analysis -- Critique Form

Speaker _____

Competencies	Part I: Message Preparation -- Appropriate for speaker, topic, audience, occasion, and purpose	M	I	S	G	E
Topic	Chooses and narrows a topic					
	Meets general purpose – to inform					
Support/ Organization	**Intro** – Uses attention-getter; identifies topic & purpose; establishes relevance & credibility; previews main points; transitions to 1ˢᵗ main point					
	Body -- *Chooses appropriate supporting material to support **each** perspective					
	*Ethically and objectively constructs an argument for each perspective					
	*Uses appropriate comparison/contrast organization & transitions (point or block method)					
	***Presentation aid** – appropriate design of advanced PowerPoint					
	Conclusion -- Restatement of thesis; memorable thought					
	Part I: Overall					
	Part II Energetic Message Delivery – Appropriate for audience, occasion, and purpose	M	I	S	G	E
Language	Uses appropriate language for the designated audience					
	Effective oral citation of sources					
Voice	**Variety** -- Uses vocal variety in volume, rate, pitch & intensity to heighten and maintain interest.					
	Accuracy -- Uses pronunciation, grammar, & articulation; minimizes filler words.					
Physical Behaviors	**Manner, movement and gestures** – Uses assertive stance; Uses movement and gestures effectively					
	Facial expression and eye contact -- Uses facial expressiveness and eye contact to support the message and engage with listeners					
	***Presentation aid** -- Effectively presents advanced PowerPoint to enhance speech (not repeat message)					
	Note cards – Effectively uses appropriately designed note cards to support speech					
Time?	Part II: Overall					

The M I S G E columns are headed: **M**issing, **I**neffective, **S**atisfactory, **G**ood, **E**xcellent   *Notes*

***Focal points for this speech** – addressed in reading and homework*
Notes – Strengths?   Areas for improvement?

Critiqued by _____

Issue Analysis -- Critique Form **Speaker** ______________

Missing, **I**neffective, **S**atisfactory, **G**ood, **E**xcellent *Notes*

Competencies	*Part I: Message Preparation -- Appropriate for speaker, topic, audience, occasion, and purpose*	M	I	S	G	E
Topic	Chooses and narrows a topic					
	Meets general purpose – to inform					
Support/ Organization	**Intro –** Uses attention-getter; identifies topic & purpose; establishes relevance & credibility; previews main points; transitions to 1st main point					
	Body -- *Chooses appropriate supporting material to support **each** perspective					
	*Ethically and objectively constructs an argument for each perspective					
	*Uses appropriate comparison/contrast organization & transitions (point or block method)					
	***Presentation aid** – appropriate design of advanced PowerPoint					
	Conclusion -- Restatement of thesis; memorable thought					
	Part I: Overall					
	Part II Energetic Message Delivery – Appropriate for audience, occasion, and purpose	**M**	**I**	**S**	**G**	**E**
Language	Uses appropriate language for the designated audience					
	Effective oral citation of sources					
Voice	**Variety** -- Uses vocal variety in volume, rate, pitch & intensity to heighten and maintain interest.					
	Accuracy -- Uses pronunciation, grammar, & articulation; minimizes filler words.					
Physical Behaviors	**Manner, movement and gestures** – Uses assertive stance; Uses movement and gestures effectively					
	Facial expression and eye contact -- Uses facial expressiveness and eye contact to support the message and engage with listeners					
	***Presentation aid --** Effectively presents advanced PowerPoint to enhance speech (not repeat message)					
	Note cards – Effectively uses appropriately designed note cards to support speech					
Time?	*Part II: Overall*					

***Focal points for this speech –** addressed in reading and homework*
Notes – Strengths? Areas for improvement?

Critiqued by ______________________

Unit V -- Persuasive Group Speech

1. Reading	*Course Guide,* Unit V Ch. 24 The Persuasive Speech Ch. 26 Organizing the Persuasive Speech Ch. 27 Special Occasion Speeches Ch. 28 Online Presentations Ch. 29 Collaborating and Presenting in Groups Ch. 30 Professional Presentations
2. Quiz	*Course Guide*; Chapters 24, 26, 27, 28, 29, 30 & Sample speeches--Canvas
3. Participation	REAL PS 5; Online and In-class activities Research participation
4. Speech	Persuasive

REAL PS 5 – Persuasive: Group Speech

Research – Research argument thoroughly

Ethics – Appeal to emotions of the audience

Analysis—Analysis of Context (Setting, Audience and Occasion)

Language/ **L**istening- Language to persuade audience; Listening for logical argument;

A persuasive speech is meant to appeal to the audience's attitudes, beliefs, and/or values and to sway the listener to the speaker's point of view. The speaker's ethical use of persuasive appeals is a vital aspect when attempting to persuade the audience of a controversial issue.

For this assignment, we'll be focusing more on structure and presentation than on content and group processes. While you may have presented in groups before, you'll have the chance to gain some strategies about making those presentations even more effective—more professional. The content and research components are reduced so that you can spend most of your time building a strong presentation. Consequently, this speech is not as heavily weighted as the others.

Speech 5- Persuasive GROUP Speech:

This speech will allow you to research a controversy of your choice and present it to your audience who might need information about the topic. Persuasive speeches use a combination of rhetorical proofs, logos, pathos, and ethos. Using a combination of these three proofs will make your speech more effective. By researching the topic using a variety of sources, your group's responsibility will be to present your topic in a clear and persuasive manner to your audience.

Persuasive speaking is a type of public speaking you will use frequently in your professional and personal life. Furthermore, group work and collaborative presentations are commonplace in the academic and professional world. Due to the added complexities of presenting information as a group, it is important for students in Public Speaking to get some practice with collaborating on group presentations!

In your major or career, you'll find that group preparation and presentation can be a very effective way to reach an audience. Traditionally group projects involve lots of time for decision-making and preparation, maybe some effort resolving conflicts, and significant presentation planning and rehearsal. College students often complain about group work because they have such difficulty meeting outside of class or even finding common areas for research if they are all in different majors. Those are realistic concerns.

For this assignment, some of that complexity has been reduced! If you usually groan when you think of group projects, relax! This one will be very useful and maybe even enjoyable!

Guidelines for Speech 5

Complexity	Level 5--- Includes levels 1, 2, 3, and 4)
Type	Persuasive Group Speech; extemporaneous
Topic Choice/focus	Controversial topic based on group interest
Audience	Audience who needs information about the issue
Purpose	Persuade
Credibility	Variety of types of sources, including library databases and local sources
Support	Examples, testimony, facts, statistics Minimum of 1 source per group member Source citation: written bibliography **and** oral citation *Note: Insufficient oral citation will result in point deduction.*
Organization	Cause-effect; problem solution; Monroe's Motivated Sequence
Voice & language	Appropriate vocal variety and persuasive language choices
Physical behavior	Mastery of technology; appropriate group interactions; transitions between group members
Presentation Aids	4-6 PowerPoint slides (plus spacer slides) Note: Each person should have at least one slide
Confidence	Building confidence
Time	7 ½-8 ½ minutes

Speech Preparation and delivery

Successful presentations will necessitate the completion of the following steps:

- **Invention**
  - Choose an appropriate topic. Think about controversies on campus, in the Town of Blacksburg, or that affect college students.
  - Develop preliminary MAP.
  - Determine audience needs.
  - Generate supporting material from a variety of sources, including your group's experience, prior knowledge and research from library databases. Research could also include primary sources.

- **Arrangement**
  - Organizational format- Monroe's Motivated Sequence
  - Create a presentation plan.

- **Style**
  - Choose persuasive language appropriate for audience
  - Choose detail appropriate for audience

- **Memory and Delivery**
  - Design and create minimum of four slides with animation (each person must have at least 1 slide). Use of spacer slides.
  - Rehearse
  - Present, using 4 x 6 note cards

Related writing

- Presentation plan and bibliography
- Critiques of peers' speeches

Topic Possibilities—Persuasive

As you consider possibilities for a controversial topic, be careful to select an issue you already know about and care about.

Brainstorm a list of at least 10 possibilities. Use the following prompts to get started:
1. List 2-3 campus issues that are of concern to your group, such as new policies, potential buildings, tuition changes, etc.
2. List 2-3 controversies that affect the Town of Blacksburg.
3. List 2-3 controversies that affect college students (loan options, graduation rates).
4. List 2-3 campus resources that VT students should be utilizing.

When your group meets to share ideas, choose a topic about which everyone in the group has some interest and experience. Merge the lists of ideas without any judgment and then discuss the possibilities one by one.

As your group makes a decision about the topic, everyone in the group should speak up to approve the topic.

Audience of Stakeholders

Once you have chosen a topic, identify the various interested groups for whom you might develop a presentation. Select a particular group and conduct an audience analysis. Your analysis of those listeners will help you decide on your main points, your research, your examples, your language, and even your organization.

Research Possibilities

Use the library databases to round out your information about the subject. Consider your group's experience and include source citations where appropriate. Your group may use any of the research methods that we have used throughout the semester.

Persuasive Speech: Presentation Plan

Your group's presentation plan and bibliography will be evaluated as part of your message preparation. Please refer to the possible organization styles from Chapter 26 in O'Hair.

MAP:

Group Members' Names:

Introduction
- **Attention**-getter
- Introduce Group topic (Clearly stating persuasive purpose)
- Motivate—Group credibility and relevance of topic to audience
- Preview persuasive thesis

Transition to next speaker & 1st main point

Body
- Use Monroe's Motivated Sequence organizational pattern (see O'Hair Chapter 26, page 375)
  - **Attention, Need, Satisfaction, Visualization, Action**
- Include well developed arguments, using claims, evidence and warrants
- Indicate sources
- Use fully developed keyword outline form
- Include transitions between EACH speaker

Transition to next speaker; signal the close of the speech (without saying "In conclusion")

Conclusion
- Summarize main points and/or reiterate persuasive claims
- Persuade audience to specific **action**

Bibliography with standard documentation format
- APA, Appendix C

Group Topic: _____

Instructor Summary of Feedback—Persuasive Group Speech

Please attach this form to your group's outline; the critique for instructor's use is on the back of this page. The outline must be available to your instructor before you can give your speech.

After your speech, your instructor will review his or her notes on a critique form and any forms that your peers complete about your speech. Your instructor might use ✓, ✓+, or ✓- on some of the lines below to show your general accomplishment in the areas listed. When the papers are returned to you, please use this form along with the instructor critique form to review your feedback. If there's something you don't understand, be sure to ask about it.

Message Preparation   (50%)_____

    Outline & Bibliography   (10%) _____

Message Delivery   (40%) _____

Speech Grade   _____

<u>Notes- Overall strengths and considerations for future speaking situations:</u>

After Public Speaking

Congratulations on your accomplishments in this course! As you continue your path toward confidence and competence in public speaking, your text could be very useful for you. You may want to keep it so that you can refresh your memory about the concepts we studied.

As you undertake assignments in other courses, please contact CommLab for support: commlab@vt.edu; www.commlab.vt.edu

Persuasive Group Speech -- Critique Form   **Group Topic:** _____

Competencies	Part I: Message Preparation -- Appropriate for speaker, topic, audience, occasion, and purpose	M	I	S	G	E	Notes
Topic	Chooses and narrows a topic						
	Meets general purpose – to persuade; connection with audience needs and interests						
Support/ Organization	**Intro** – Uses attention-getter; identifies topic & purpose; establishes relevance & credibility; previews main points; transitions to 1ˢᵗ main point						
	Body – Provides appropriate supporting material with vivid, specific detail						
	*__Transitions__ between group members: S1 S2 S3 S4						
	*__Persuasive appeals__ – ethos, logos, pathos						
	*__Organization__ – Uses appropriate pattern (Monroe's: Need, Satisfaction, Visualization)						
	Presentation aids – Consistency & design of effective PPT						
	Conclusion – Emphasizes call to action; impact						
	Part I: Overall Message Preparation						
	Part II __Energetic__ Message Delivery – Appropriate for audience, occasion, and purpose	M	I	S	G	E	
Language	*Uses appropriate and **persuasive** language appropriate to designated audience.						
	*__Oral citation of sources__ (1 per group member) S1 S2 S3 S4						
Voice	**Variety** – Overall variety in volume, rate, pitch & intensity to heighten and maintain interest.						
	Accuracy – Overall use of pronunciation, grammar, & articulation; minimizes filler words.						
Physical Behaviors	*__Group enthusiasm and interaction; attentiveness__ to group members when speaking						
	Appearance – Appropriate dress of group members						
	Movement and gestures – Overall use of effective movement and gestures						
	Facial expression and eye contact – Overall use of facial expressiveness and eye contact to support the message and engage with listeners						
	*__Presentation aids__ – Overall use of effective PPT to enhance speech (1 slide per group member) S1 S2 S3 S4						
Time?	*Part II: Overall Message Delivery*						

__Focal points for this speech__ – addressed in reading and homework. Strengths? Areas for improvement?

Persuasive Group Speech -- Critique Form   **Group Topic: _____**

Competencies	Part I: Message Preparation -- Appropriate for speaker, topic, audience, occasion, and purpose	M	I	S	G	E
Topic	Chooses and narrows a topic					
	Meets general purpose – to persuade; connection with audience needs and interests					
Support/ Organization	**Intro** – Uses attention-getter; identifies topic & purpose; establishes relevance & credibility; previews main points; transitions to 1ˢᵗ main point					
	Body – Provides appropriate supporting material with vivid, specific detail					
	*Transitions between group members: S1 S2 S3 S4					
	*Persuasive appeals – ethos, logos, pathos					
	*Organization – Uses appropriate pattern (Monroe's: Need, Satisfaction, Visualization)					
	Presentation aids – Consistency & design of effective PPT					
	Conclusion – Emphasizes call to action; impact					
	Part I: Overall Message Preparation					
	Part II Energetic Message Delivery – Appropriate for audience, occasion, and purpose	M	I	S	G	E
Language	*Uses appropriate and **persuasive** language appropriate to designated audience.					
	*Oral citation of sources (1 per group member) S1 S2 S3 S4					
Voice	**Variety** – Overall variety in volume, rate, pitch & intensity to heighten and maintain interest.					
	Accuracy – Overall use of pronunciation, grammar, & articulation; minimizes filler words.					
Physical Behaviors	*Group enthusiasm and interaction; attentiveness to group members when speaking					
	Appearance – Appropriate dress of group members					
	Movement and gestures – Overall use of effective movement and gestures					
	Facial expression and eye contact – Overall use of facial expressiveness and eye contact to support the message and engage with listeners					
	*Presentation aids – Overall use of effective PPT to enhance speech (1 slide per group member) S1 S2 S3 S4					
Time?	*Part II: Overall Message Delivery*					

Missing, Ineffective, Satisfactory, Good, Excellent   *Notes*

*** Focal points for this speech** – addressed in reading and homework. Strengths? Areas for improvement?*

Critiqued by _____

Persuasive Group Speech -- Critique Form   Group Topic: _____

Competencies	Part I: Message Preparation -- Appropriate for speaker, topic, audience, occasion, and purpose	M	I	S	G	E
Topic	Chooses and narrows a topic					
	Meets general purpose – to persuade; connection with audience needs and interests					
Support/ Organization	**Intro** – Uses attention-getter; identifies topic & purpose; establishes relevance & credibility; previews main points; transitions to 1ˢᵗ main point					
	Body – Provides appropriate supporting material with vivid, specific detail					
	*****Transitions** between group members: S1 S2 S3 S4					
	*****Persuasive appeals** – ethos, logos, pathos					
	*****Organization** – Uses appropriate pattern (Monroe's: Need, Satisfaction, Visualization)					
	Presentation aids – Consistency & design of effective PPT					
	Conclusion – Emphasizes call to action; impact					
	Part I: Overall Message Preparation					
	Part II Energetic Message Delivery – Appropriate for audience, occasion, and purpose	M	I	S	G	E
Language	*Uses appropriate and **persuasive** language appropriate to designated audience.					
	*****Oral citation of sources** (1 per group member) S1 S2 S3 S4					
Voice	**Variety** – Overall variety in volume, rate, pitch & intensity to heighten and maintain interest.					
	Accuracy – Overall use of pronunciation, grammar, & articulation; minimizes filler words.					
Physical Behaviors	*****Group enthusiasm and interaction; attentiveness** to group members when speaking					
	Appearance – Appropriate dress of group members					
	Movement and gestures – Overall use of effective movement and gestures					
	Facial expression and eye contact – Overall use of facial expressiveness and eye contact to support the message and engage with listeners					
	*****Presentation aids** – Overall use of effective PPT to enhance speech (1 slide per group member) S1 S2 S3 S4					
Time?	*Part II: Overall Message Delivery*					

Missing, Ineffective, Satisfactory, Good, Excellent   Notes

***Focal points for this speech** – addressed in reading and homework Strengths? Areas for improvement?*

Critiqued by _____

Persuasive Group Speech -- Critique Form

Group Topic: _____

Missing, Ineffective, Satisfactory, Good, Excellent   *Notes*

Competencies	*Part I: Message Preparation -- Appropriate for speaker, topic, audience, occasion, and purpose*	M	I	S	G	E
Topic	Chooses and narrows a topic					
	Meets general purpose – to persuade; connection with audience needs and interests					
Support/ Organization	**Intro –** Uses attention-getter; identifies topic & purpose; establishes relevance & credibility; previews main points; transitions to 1ˢᵗ main point					
	Body – Provides appropriate supporting material with vivid, specific detail					
	*****Transitions** between group members: S1 S2 S3 S4					
	*****Persuasive appeals** – ethos, logos, pathos					
	*****Organization** – Uses appropriate pattern (Monroe's: Need, Satisfaction, Visualization)					
	Presentation aids – Consistency & design of effective PPT					
	Conclusion – Emphasizes call to action; impact					
	Part I: Overall Message Preparation					
	*Part II **Energetic** Message Delivery – Appropriate for audience, occasion, and purpose*	M	I	S	G	E
Language	*Uses appropriate and **persuasive** language appropriate to designated audience.					
	*****Oral citation of sources** (1 per group member) S1 S2 S3 S4					
Voice	**Variety** – Overall variety in volume, rate, pitch & intensity to heighten and maintain interest.					
	Accuracy – Overall use of pronunciation, grammar, & articulation; minimizes filler words.					
Physical Behaviors	*****Group enthusiasm and interaction; attentiveness** to group members when speaking					
	Appearance – Appropriate dress of group members					
	Movement and gestures – Overall use of effective movement and gestures					
	Facial expression and eye contact – Overall use of facial expressiveness and eye contact to support the message and engage with listeners					
	*****Presentation aids** – Overall use of effective PPT to enhance speech (1 slide per group member) S1 S2 S3 S4					
Time?	*Part II: Overall Message Delivery*					

*****Focal points for this speech** –addressed in reading and homework. Strengths? Areas for improvement?*

Critiqued by _____

Persuasive Group Speech -- Critique Form

Group Topic: _____

Missing, Ineffective, Satisfactory, Good, Excellent *Notes*

Competencies	Part I: Message Preparation -- Appropriate for speaker, topic, audience, occasion, and purpose	M	I	S	G	E
Topic	Chooses and narrows a topic					
	Meets general purpose – to persuade; connection with audience needs and interests					
Support/ Organization	**Intro** – Uses attention-getter; identifies topic & purpose; establishes relevance & credibility; previews main points; transitions to 1ˢᵗ main point					
	Body – Provides appropriate supporting material with vivid, specific detail					
	***Transitions** between group members: S1 S2 S3 S4					
	***Persuasive appeals** – ethos, logos, pathos					
	***Organization** – Uses appropriate pattern (Monroe's: Need, Satisfaction, Visualization)					
	Presentation aids – Consistency & design of effective PPT					
	Conclusion – Emphasizes call to action; impact					
	Part I: Overall Message Preparation					
	Part II **Energetic** Message Delivery – Appropriate for audience, occasion, and purpose	M	I	S	G	E
Language	*Uses appropriate and **persuasive** language appropriate to designated audience.					
	***Oral citation of sources** (1 per group member) S1 S2 S3 S4					
Voice	**Variety** – Overall variety in volume, rate, pitch & intensity to heighten and maintain interest.					
	Accuracy – Overall use of pronunciation, grammar, & articulation; minimizes filler words.					
Physical Behaviors	***Group enthusiasm and interaction; attentiveness** to group members when speaking					
	Appearance – Appropriate dress of group members					
	Movement and gestures – Overall use of effective movement and gestures					
	Facial expression and eye contact – Overall use of facial expressiveness and eye contact to support the message and engage with listeners					
	***Presentation aids** – Overall use of effective PPT to enhance speech (1 slide per group member) S1 S2 S3 S4					
Time?	*Part II: Overall Message Delivery*					

*****Focal points for this speech** – addressed in reading and homework. Strengths? Areas for improvement?*

Critiqued by _____

Appendix A: Supplementary Notes

The instructors in this course work hard to establish consistency across sections. Consequently, they include these notes at some point during the semester so that all students have an equal opportunity to succeed. The following notes include reminders about course norms that will help you to be successful in your speeches.

1. Building Credibility

One way to motivate your audience is to establish credibility, and reference to that credibility should be included in the intro. Your credibility might be based on your character, your connection with the audience, and/or your expertise on a subject. Listeners need to know why they should believe you whether you're informing them or persuading them.

A good credibility statement includes a person's expertise and personal attachment to a topic. For example, "As president of the fraternity/project manager/group leader, I have been overseeing and planning this project since its inception last year."

O'Hair offers a good checklist on p. 357, which includes 5 tips for establishing credibility.

2. Citing Sources

Audiences WANT to know that you have support for your ideas. Let them know the sources of your information! Citing sources not only helps to build your credibility as an ethical researcher and speaker, but these citations also protect you from plagiarizing.

Plagiarism is a violation of the University Honor Code, and violations will be reported.

Planning for citations -- outline and bibliography
- In your outline, note the points at which citations will occur in the speech. Make a parenthetical reference on the outline; for example (Preston, 2018).
- You also need to include a bibliography at the end of your speech outline. Use standard format -- usually MLA or APA; see O'Hair Appendices or library website

Oral citations
Provide enough information to persuade the listener that you've chosen high-quality sources. Consider the types the sources that will be most meaningful to your listeners. Include the following:
- Author or origin of source (on the National Science Foundation website); Use author's name ONLY if the listener would recognize the name – Donald Trump, for example.
- Type of source (journal article, textbook, interview, lecture notes, documentary, etc.)
- Title of source (*A Speaker's Guidebook*)
- Year published (this shows the audience the currency of your information)

An oral citation might sound like this: "According to the *mission statement* on TED website, updated in 2018, 'TED Talks are ideas worth sharing.'"

3. Visual Support

Appearance Choices -- Your choice of dress depends on the context of your speech: the purpose, the time of day, the setting, and the identity of your audience. Your audience will see you and react to your appearance before they hear your first word and begin to process your message. Be sure that your appearance meets the expectations of your audience and enhances your credibility!

- Plan your appearance ahead of time -- just as you plan any message you intend for an audience.
- Generally, you should dress in a slightly more formal way than your audience. When you present a story to your classmates, you should look like a college student so that you enhance your connection with your audience. If you wear your prom dress or your interview suit, that connection with your audience will be lessened. Of course, if you are returning to your high school to discuss interview skills with high school seniors, then your interview suit is appropriate.
- Choose clothes/accessories that are comfortable and won't distract you (or the audience) with slipping zippers, bare stomachs, or annoying jangling. **No hats!** Aside from being unprofessional, they shade your face and obscure your expressions.
- Whatever you choose, be sure that your clothes are clean and neat.

Presentation Aids -- Strategies -- Generally, the term "presentation aids" includes any visual or auditory support you might use to enhance your speech -- PowerPoint, transparencies, music, a movie. Your text offers good suggestions about developing these aids, so the following list of considerations is offered to complement -- not repeat -- that list. These considerations reflect the philosophy of this particular course and are important for your success:

- Avoid repeating points in your speech on your PowerPoint slide.
  - o You've seen many teachers who provide bulleted lists of points; students write down the points, and the faculty member uses the list as a guide for the lecture. This repetition of the speech may work in a teaching setting -- one in which students are expected to copy and learn exact words. However, in most other settings, this is a boring use of visual support.
  - o Instead, use the visual to enhance (not repeat) your speech. Use pictures, charts, or graphs with legible and large labels and titles.
- Cite the source for any materials (charts, graphs) you've borrowed from journals or books. You can list the source at the bottom of the slide.
- Show the slide only when it fits with your speech. Create blank or spacer slides between the slides you want the audience to see. Use the same template as you've chosen for the rest of your presentation, but include no writing or pictures.
- Use these blank slides to pace your presentation. Without blank slides, speakers must either force the audience to view a slide related to a previous point (thus distracting them from the new point being discussed) or race on to the next point only because the next slide is exposed. Don't let your PowerPoint slide control you!
- No title slide is necessary. Your introduction should generate audience interest and explain the focus of your speech.
- When you're using a presentation aid, maintain eye contact with your audience; keep your body turned to your audience.

Appendix B: Alternative to Research Participation

You may complete one of the following options as an alternative to the required research participation. (Any of the activities below should take approximately 1-2 hours of your time – more time than the research participation would take.) Of course, aside from meeting a requirement, these activities will help to enrich your understanding of communication research and/or public speaking specifically.

This alternative must be submitted before the end of Unit V.

I. Analysis of Self as Speaker

Review of one of your own speeches in CommLab (Room 2034 Newman Library). Meet with a CommLab coach who can either record your speech or watch a recording of one of your speeches that was created in class. See your teacher for your speech recording.

1. Complete a critique form as you discuss the presentation with the coach. (Next page)
2. Respond to the analysis questions on the back of the form (Note: The CommLab coach will share observations with you, but YOU must complete the form and the analysis questions.)
3. Submit as required by your instructor

II. Speaker Analysis

Your personal public speaking skills can be enhanced every time you critically observe a speech presentation. You are exercising those skills in class, but it's also helpful to observe and analyze speeches that are delivered in other settings and speeches that are recorded, thus offering you the opportunity to replay parts of the speech.

Review a professional speaker who is visiting campus. (Instructor approval is required.) Review process --

1. Complete a critique form (next page)
2. Respond to the analysis questions on the back of the form
3. Submit as required by your instructor

Speaker Analysis -- Critique Form

1. Speaker _____

2. Speech occasion _____ **date of speech** _____

3. Speech setting _____

Missing, Ineffective, Satisfactory, Good, Excellent *Notes*

Competencies	*Part I: Message Preparation*	M	I	S	G	E
Topic	Chooses and narrows a topic appropriate for audience and occasion.					
Thesis/ Specific Purpose	Communicates the thesis/specific purpose in a manner appropriate for the audience and occasion.					
Support	Provides supporting material appropriate for the audience and occasion.					
	Develops appropriate presentation aids					
Organization	Uses an organization pattern appropriate to topic, audience, occasion & purpose.					
	Part I: Overall					
	Part II Message Delivery					
Language	Uses language that is appropriate to the audience, occasion & purpose.					
Vocal Variety	Uses vocal variety in rate, pitch & intensity to heighten and maintain interest.					
Vocal Accuracy	Uses pronunciation, grammar, & articulation appropriate to the designated audience.					
Physical Behaviors	Uses physical behaviors (movement & gestures) that support the verbal message.					
	Uses facial expressiveness and eye contact to support the verbal message.					
	Implements presentation aids effectively					
Time?	*Part II: Overall*					

Notes:

Attach ticket/program for any speech that you attended on campus. If you review your speech in CommLab (Room 2034 Newman Library), a CommLab coach should sign this critique form. After you complete this form, respond to analysis questions on back, and then submit the analysis to your instructor.

Submitted by _____

Speech analysis

1. What was the speaker's MAP? How well did he or she fulfill the promise of the MAP?

2. List three strengths of the speech. Provide examples from the speech.

3. List three suggestions for improvement. Provide examples from the speech and cite references in the O'Hair text that would be helpful for each area.

4. How could this speech relate to a speaking task that you'll undertake as a student or as an employee? What strategies might be useful to you in the future?

5. Using the grading criteria described earlier in this *Course Guide*, what grade would you give this speech? Why?

Appendix C: Course Development

Traditional Models of Public Speaking

Every college and university in the country offers some version of Public Speaking. Faculty have struggled over the years to find a good mix of theory and practice, to appropriately incorporate technology, and to meet the needs of students across a wide variety of majors. Some offer Public Speaking online; students tape speeches and send them in for a grade. Although this approach reduces the cost of offering the course and certainly makes the most of technology, it can't offer the kind of speaking experience that can be found in a speech classroom with a teacher and an audience. Some of those online models do include classroom speeches, but the support for speech development is not available. In other models, instruction is provided in a large lecture, and the speech practice is conducted in smaller sections. This model can be effective, but the amount of lecture and theory can sometimes confuse students who are juggling different teachers and expectations between the large lecture and the smaller recitation sections. Other institutions offer Public Speaking in standard 3-hour-per-week courses with numerous instructors, whose instruction may vary significantly from section to section.

Designing a New Model

At Virginia Tech, we spent nine months planning and preparing for the birth of our new public speaking model. Faculty in the Department of Communication started exploring possibilities in Fall 2005 by considering the various models offered by other institutions and their own experiences teaching Public Speaking at this university. They also discussed the role of the course with faculty in other majors -- those whose students take the course -- so that we could be sure the course would meet the needs of students in various majors.

The team of faculty began sketching out a course that would focus on informative speaking across a semester. Dr. Marlene M. Preston designed the Interchange Model--a delivery mechanism that capitalized on (1) the technology available at Virginia Tech, (2) contemporary learning theory, and (3) the "REAL PS" concept that serves as the thread tying all speech assignments together: Research, Ethics, Analysis/Audience and Listening/Language.

A grant from Virginia Tech's Center for Excellence in Undergraduate Teaching allowed further planning in Spring 2006 and a pilot program in Summer 2006. Preston, Matt Giglio, and Kristin English worked on text selection and various aspects of the course development.

The course design has been implemented fully since Fall 2006. Faculty and students alike have found that the course has worked well to meet a wide range of student needs.

The Interchange

Preston's *Interchange Model* capitalizes on the kinds of instructional activities that can be best used online and the kinds that make the best use of classroom time.

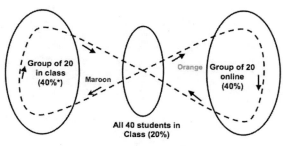

*Percentages indicate the approximate amount of time students spend in each area of the course.

This allows for an efficient discussion of course policies and upcoming units. At other times, half of the class (the Maroon group) heads for an *online loop* of the course while the other half of the class (the Orange group) is preparing and delivering speeches in the *classroom loop*.

The Maroons and Oranges develop separate identities and communities as they work together over the semester. Thus, a student delivers a speech in a supportive environment to a smaller number of students who have become a learning community.

Results and Ongoing Revision

Students reported greater satisfaction with the new model and also greater appreciation of the subject matter. They appreciated the convenience of the course and recognized the real-world applications of the strategies they learned.

Instructor and student feedback is used each semester to increasingly enhance the course.

Administration and Further Development

2009 – present
- Ms. Brandi Quesenberry, Course Director & *Course Guide* editor
- Dr. Marlene Preston, *Course Guide* author

2007 – 2009
- Ms. Britta Long, Course Coordinator
- Dr. Marlene Preston, Course Director & *Course Guide* author

2006 – 2007
- Mr. Matt Giglio, Course Coordinator
- Dr. Marlene Preston, Course Director & *Course Guide* author

Note: *Dr. Preston shares proceeds from the sale of the Course Guide to support CommLab, equipment costs, GTA development, and other expenses related to the building of students' oral communication skills.*